THE
INNER RUNNER

THE
INNER RUNNER

Running to a More
Successful, Creative, and
Confident You

JASON R. KARP, PHD

Skyhorse Publishing

Skyhorse Publishing books may be purchased in bulk at special discounts for sales promotion, corporate gifts, fund-raising, or educational purposes. Special editions can also be created to specifications. For details, contact the Special Sales Department, Skyhorse Publishing, 307 West 36th Street, 11th Floor, New York, NY 10018 or info@skyhorsepublishing.com.

Skyhorse® and Skyhorse Publishing® are registered trademarks of Skyhorse Publishing, Inc.®, a Delaware corporation.

Visit our website at www.skyhorsepublishing.com.

10 9 8 7 6 5 4 3 2 1

Library of Congress Cataloging-in-Publication Data is available on file.

Cover design by Tom Lau
Cover photo credit iStockphoto

ISBN: 978-1-63450-795-0
Ebook ISBN: 978-1-63450-801-8

Printed in the United States of America

To my father, Monroe, whose long walking strides caused me to run to keep up. And to my mother, Muriel, who always encouraged me to pursue my dreams. They are both with me with every step I run. In my parents' memory, ten percent of my profit on every book sold will be donated to charity—the American Heart Association in my father's memory and Susan G. Komen for the Cure in my mother's memory.

CONTENTS

ACKNOWLEDGEMENTS

This book, the subject of which has been on my mind ever since I became a runner, wouldn't have earned a place on a bookshelf without the support of many people, primary among them my agent, Grace Freedson. I thank her for understanding my ambition and my crazy persistence, and for providing me with the opportunity to share my thoughts and deep passion with the world.

I also thank the team at Skyhorse, including Bill Wolfsthal, Julie Ganz, and Brittney Soldano and cover designer Tom Lau; all of the runners I have met, or run with, or coached over the years, who have taught me so much about the sport and the running life; Jennifer Zerling for confirming the idea to write this book; and the people who have shared their remarkable and inspiring stories, including B.J. (Bedford) Miller, Ronnie Goodman, Walter Herzog, Cody Johnson, Kristin Stehly, and Sabrina Walker. This book is richer for their contributions. Each of them, in different ways, has embodied what the inner runner is all about, and the world is a better place because of them.

Finally, I thank the most talented writer I know—my twin brother, Jack, for his honest feedback on the first draft of the manuscript and for inspiring me to view my book as a piece of art and do more with my writing than tell a story.

PREFACE

runner

[ruhn-er]

noun

AN ANIMAL THAT GOES QUICKLY BY MOVING THE LEGS MORE
RAPIDLY THAN AT A WALK AND IN SUCH A MANNER THAT FOR
AN INSTANT IN EACH STEP ALL FEET ARE OFF THE GROUND.

Running is one of the oldest physical activities. Long before the beginning of modern civilization, our ancestors raced through woodlands and prairies, chasing wild animals to feed their families. Running, and being able to run long and fast, was very important.

Many thousands of years later, we have become fascinated by running (and its walking predecessor), one example of which is illustrated by parents' joy at their child's first steps. A child's ability to walk is deemed so important that we label this occasion a milestone and document the exact day the child's first steps are taken. This ability to walk, and eventually to run, is met with even more joy from the children themselves when they discover the freedom that it confers. We have all seen the smile on a child's face when he or she runs around the playground.

Many of those boys and girls go on to play organized sports, for most of which running is the foundation. Nearly every sport requires at least some running, and of the few that don't—like golf, diving, or ice hockey—running is an important, effective part of the athlete's fitness training. Walk onto any college campus, and it won't take long to find out that the most aerobically fit students are the runners on the cross-country team, and the most anaerobically fit students are the sprinters and jumpers on the track-and-field team.

Many coaches in other sports make their athletes run, because they recognize its effectiveness for improving fitness. Unfortunately, some coaches and old-school physical education teachers use running as a form of punishment, making their athletes and students run laps or "suicides" on the school's basketball court, instead of using running as a way to improve their athletes' fitness and teach them how to deal with discomfort. All athletes can learn a lot from running.

Watching young children run around the playground, it is evident that something special is taking place when we move on two legs. Indeed, it is a form of locomotion that makes humans unique from most other animals. There is no shortage of scientists studying running from every possible angle— physiological, biochemical, anatomical, biomechanical, medical, psychological, evolutionary, cognitive, and emotional. Not only is bipedal running unique, how humans think about running and about themselves as runners is also unique.

The reason that humans are the only animals that think about running is, of course, the size and complexity of our brains. Unlike even our nearest mammalian ancestors—

apes and monkeys—humans have the ability to look inward and think about themselves, their place in the world, and how to improve their characteristics. Unlike other animals, we are aware of our own mind, our own soul, and our own emotions. And that gives us a tremendous amount of power and responsibility.

If the fields of physical education and exercise science were ever asked to come up with a slogan, a front runner would likely be a line borrowed from the ancient Roman poet Juvenal: *"Mens sana in corpore sano"*—a sound mind in a sound body. Indeed, many runners seem to support this sentiment with a zeal that approaches the fanatical.

For me, the fanatics started thirty-two years ago, during the Presidential Physical Fitness Tests in fifth grade. Remember those? Two of the tests were the 50-yard dash and 600-meter run. I ran the 50 in 7.3 seconds and the 600 in two minutes and one second. It was then that I discovered that I had some talent, although I wasn't the quickest in my class. But I was close. It was also then that I discovered the freedom that running confers. Little did I know how much it would change my life. I became a runner, and there was no turning back. Some things, once they get started, are impossible to stop.

It was not much later, during an innocent race once around the track in sixth grade on my middle-school track team, that I also discovered that running can be physically uncomfortable. Midway through the final curve of that 400-meter race, I felt something, something that would also change my life. Her name, I learned much later, was Lactate. As I continued to sprint around the track that day, she teased me with her power, drawing on the reigns, gently at first, then harder with each passing moment. Harder. Harder. By the time I had reached the finish line, she had taken control of my whole body with her rapture. I could no longer move. It was love at first sight. My love affair with running and Lactate has continued all these years.

Running may be simple, but it is also extremely complex, because human beings are complex. And that's what makes running so interesting. It allows us to look inward—at the inner runner—to find out who we really are and embrace the challenge of discovering our true selves. Sometimes we find out things we don't want to know. Not every time I have run a race do I cross the finish line feeling like I gave it everything I had. There have been many times I have felt guilty, that I knew there was something else I could have done in that race that I did not do. It bothers me, because I feel like I have failed myself. Sometimes that happens in life. We fail ourselves. But also like life, we often have another chance.

Few other times in our lives are we faced with such decisive moments. Every time you approach the starting line of a race, you know you're going to be faced with that. It causes some anxiety, which explains why runners take multiple trips to the bathroom in the moments before a race.

In nearly every way, including my relationship with the bathroom, my life has been defined by running. Every aspect of it is somehow influenced by being a runner. When I speak, when I write, when I coach, and, of course, when I run. Everything I do, how I carry myself, is all influenced by running. Not running means not being me. It's remarkable that millions of other runners feel the same way. Wouldn't it be great if all runners could articulate the thoughts and feelings they experience on their runs and what they become through running? In *The Inner Runner*, I try to do just that. Why are so many people drawn to running? Why does it have so much impact on me and on so many others? What is it about running that empowers so many people? And how can runners harness that power to create a more meaningful life? *The Inner Runner* addresses these questions and a whole lot more. I wrote a whole book to explain to myself the answers to these questions.

No matter how long my to-do list is, how much stress I'm feeling, or how much ambition I have, when I'm outside running, none of it matters. Everything stops—the work, the stress, the to-dos, the relationships, the everything. Running is my "me" time, and everything and everyone else can wait. There's no place I'd rather be. I don't feel bad about it, and I don't apologize for it. There are few things in life, and I mean *very* few, that prevent me from running, that take that "me" time away. It's just me and the road, or me and the track, or me and the trail. It's me and my consciousness and me and my subconscious. It's me and my sweat, me and my effort. What effort will I put forth today? What awaits me on my run?

Most people, especially non-runners, are unaware of how running affects our whole lives. It affects life in both obvious and subtle ways. The obvious, of course, is that running makes us healthier, gives us sculpted legs, and places us among the most aerobically fit people on the planet. The subtle, while less obvious by definition, is no less important. Running has taught me how to succeed, how to fail, how to win, and how to lose. It has taught me discipline. It has taught me devotion. It has taught me how to strive for the things I want. It has taught me that I better do the work if I want to be successful. It has taught me to be patient (although I'm still working on that!). It has taught me that I don't always get what I want. It can teach you those things, too. I really hope that running fills you up the way it fills me up, every day of my life, so that you, too, can find out who you are and what you can become.

In addition to the many documented physical benefits of running (and there really are so many that it's fair to say that running may be the single best thing you can do for your health), there are numerous psychological, emotional, cognitive, and spiritual benefits. (Some ultra-endurance runners—those who run very long distances—claim they even find God when they run.) This book explores many of these benefits, right down to (and up to) your brain.

The Inner Runner is not about how to run a faster 5K or train for a marathon in twenty weeks; there are more than enough books to cover that, including a few of my own. And they all miss the point, including mine. Ultimately, running is not about getting faster, not for most of us, anyway. Getting faster is an outcome. Running is not about outcomes. It is about a very special, even holy, process that blends the physical with the philosophical, the egotistical with the emotional. And so this book takes a different view of running, examining how running affects every part of our lives and how all of the parts are intimately interconnected to each other and the whole person. It explores what it means to be a runner, how the simple act of putting one foot in front of the other helps you become a better person and provides a path to a more meaningful, more creative, more imaginative, more productive, more confident, more healthful, and more successful life. *The Inner Runner* is as much about life as it is about running.

Although prefaces appear at the beginning of books, they are usually written last, after the author has had time to reflect on what he or she has written. The concept of *The Inner Runner* began as a session I led at a fitness industry conference in 2011. I took conference attendees on a run through Torrey Pines State Reserve in La Jolla, California, talking about the emotional and philosophical aspects of running. Since that first conference, I have held the session a few more times in various locations in the US and around the world, each time trying to get closer to the meaning that I want to convey. After a friend experienced the session at one of the conferences, she said, "You know, you should write a book about that."

When I began the journey of writing this book, I wanted to capture the essence of those conference sessions, but I didn't know much of what I was going to write. I wanted it to be an experience, not just for the reader, but also for myself. As social theorist and philosopher Michel Foucault wrote, "If I had to write a book to communicate what I have already thought, I'd never have the courage to begin it . . . When I write, I do it above all to change myself and not think the same as before."

As I reflect on what I have written on the pages that follow and try to make sense of it all, I can honestly say that I do not think the same as before. I find myself humbled by what running really means and what it really does for us. For many, running is a pathway to experiences and emotions that cannot always be articulated. It is often hard to explain with words how I feel when I race or when I see one of the runners I coach have a breakthrough. It is a feeling deep inside of me. I have tried on these pages to articulate what it means to experience what running gives us, how it molds us into better, more deeply conscious people, just as the miles and interval workouts mold us into faster, more enduring runners. Sometimes, I believe I have succeeded in articulating these things; other times, I feel I am still far away. Runners share a secret that cannot easily be expressed: You don't become a runner and then run. You run and run and run, and then begin to understand what it means to be a runner. Sometimes, there just is no satisfying way to articulate that. It must be felt.

WHY DO WE RUN?

"IT IS ONE OF THE ONLY THINGS IN LIFE
I HAVE FOUND TO BE TRULY FAIR."

In the couple of years prior to running in the 2008 US Olympic Marathon Trials in New York, Jon Little was training in Kansas City, Missouri, where he was attending law school. He ran 90 to 100 miles per week on a regular basis, once going over 120, and ran twice per day nearly every day, while juggling classes on legal reasoning and civil procedure. His alarm was set for 5:30 a.m. for his morning runs.

When his alarm buzzed, Jon didn't hit the snooze button like so many other people do. Instead, he rolled himself out of bed and fell onto the hardwood floor. This was his daily ritual to wake himself up and force himself to run before going to class. "Once I hit the floor, I knew I would get out of bed," he says matter-of-factly. It was dark and 20 degrees outside.

Why did Jon do this every day of his life? He certainly didn't need to. He was already on his way to becoming a lawyer. In high school, he was a 4:19 miler and 9:42 two-miler and ran on two NCAA Division I university teams, running 8:25 for 3,000 meters and 14:45 for 5,000 meters, excellent times for any runner. He could have put his running shoes away after graduating college or continued to keep running recreationally to stay fit and sane while spending countless hours in the law library. He certainly didn't need to get up at 5:30 a.m. every day and run more miles than he had ever run before.

Why do we run? It depends on whom you ask.

If you were to ask someone who doesn't run why we run, he might say, "You're crazy. You shouldn't run. It's bad for your knees."

If you were to ask a zoologist why we run, he might say we run because we are animals, and that's what animals evolved to do. Running is essential to an animal's life. Animals run to hunt; they run because they're being hunted; they run to play; they run out of panic; and they even run to flirt with and show off to other members of their species. The zoologist may be right—on playgrounds across the country, human animals show off their speed, as boys and girls race each other during recess.

If you were to ask a physiologist why we run, he might say we run because we have running bodies: running hearts, running lungs, running muscles, running bones, running glands. Without a long ancestry of running, these bodily structures would not be what they are and would not function as they do. *Homo sapiens* is a land animal.

Throughout a long racial history, *Homo sapiens* has had to depend upon himself whenever he wanted to go somewhere, and sometimes he wanted to go somewhere in a hurry. He had to run, and by running he became a man who runs. Had he stuck to walking, he would now be quite physically different. His heart never would have reached the maximum stroke volume of 200 milliliters of blood per beat, nor the maximum rate of 190 or more beats per minute that a trained, young-adult runner's heart can reach. His muscles never would have developed the 60,000 miles of capillaries that surround them, like intricate spiderwebs to deliver oxygen. His lungs never would have developed such a thin wall over such an enormous area to become the perfect medium for oxygen and carbon dioxide gas exchange. His eccrine glands never would have developed into such efficient sweat producers that enable rapid evaporation and the ability to stay cool in very hot environments. The physiologist would argue that our bodies are exquisitely made for running, especially long distances.

If you were to ask an overweight person why we run, he might say we run because it is the best way to burn calories and lose weight. And he'd be right. Research shows that, on a minute-by-minute basis, running burns more calories than any other physical activity, with the possible exception of cross-country skiing. And because the weight-bearing nature of running is dangerous for an overweight body, running has the effect of getting rid of weight fast to protect one's joints from damage. So if you want to lose weight quickly and keep it off, it pays to become a runner. Or at least someone who runs.

If you were to ask a historian why we run, he might say we run because running is deep in our social history. The earliest known running races date back to about 2035 BC in ancient Sumer. In ancient Greece, commonly regarded as the birthplace of competitive sport, running was a highly regarded physical trait. Most runners are familiar with the legendary run of the Greek messenger Pheidippides from the battleground of Marathon to the marketplace in Athens to announce the Greeks' war victory. It is from that starting point of his run in Greece that we get the name of the race that has become a prominent item on people's bucket lists. But Pheidippides isn't the only historic runner. All ancient peoples have such tales of great running. The Inca civilization had no horses or other animals for rapid transportation. Messages were sent by relay runners, each of whom ran about a mile in distance, carrying knotted ropes to refresh their memories of the details they were to transmit by word of mouth. The extensive system of unpaved roads throughout the widespread Inca territory, totaling 14,000 miles, was entirely for travel by foot, especially running. Much of this running was done at 9,000 feet or more of elevation over the Andes mountains, a perfect height for the development of aerobic endurance.

If you were to ask a sociologist why we run, he might say we run to satisfy society's basic need for self-fulfillment—in the arts, in exploration of the earth, of outer space, and of the inner space within the individual self. Every sound society must have a foundation of what can be called "moral energy," of courage and will to begin and maintain the development of energies and talents toward their highest potentials, despite all fear of danger, exhaustion, ridicule, and failure. Inconsequential as running may seem in our society, what more available, more healthful, more developmental, more satisfying activity do we have to meet this universal need for self-affirmation?

If you were to ask a psychologist why we run, he might say we run because it's satisfying, that it is just as, if not more, effective as prescription drugs in ameliorating symptoms of depression, that it affects our brains and our minds in ways we are still learning about, and that it provides a sense of achievement for its own sake. He might reference Albert Bandura's self-efficacy theory and tell us that running increases and reinforces our beliefs in our own capabilities and makes us feel good about ourselves.

If you were to ask Roger Bannister, the world's first sub-four-minute miler, why we run, you might find his answer among the pages of his book, *The Four-Minute Mile*: "I find in running—win or lose—a deep satisfaction that I cannot express in any other way . . . I sometimes think that running has given me a glimpse of the greatest freedom that a man can ever know, because it results in the simultaneous liberation of both body and mind."

If you were to ask a theologian why we run, he might say we run for spiritual reasons, that through our physical efforts, we bring ourselves closer to God. When God created Adam and Eve, he gave them bodies and biology most suitable for running, and when we run, we glorify God by living the way God intended. The theologian would further point out that the Bible has a number of references to running, like in the book of Hebrews (12:1): ". . . and let us run with endurance the race that is set before us."

If you were to ask Dr. George Sheehan, the late cardiologist and running philosopher—whom I had the privilege to meet at a 10K race in Asbury Park, New Jersey in 1993—why we run, his answer might be the wisest one yet: "I run so I do not lose the me I was yesterday and the me I might become tomorrow."

If you were to ask a Greek taxicab driver in Rosemont, Illinois why we run, his answer might surprise you. In the spring of 2007, I was sitting in the back of a taxicab in Rosemont, Illinois, just outside of Chicago. I was in town to speak at a fitness-industry conference. I brought my racing shoes and clothes, because I planned to run a race in Chicago's Grant Park while I was there. I didn't have a car in Rosemont, so I got up extra early and took a taxi from the hotel to the park. When I stepped into the taxi, rubbing the early morning from my eyes, the taxicab driver asked in an accent I couldn't quite place, "Where are you going?"

"Grant Park in Chicago," I responded. "Going to run a race."

The taxicab driver immediately got excited. "When I was back home in Greece, I used to run all over the country!" he exclaimed, sounding like he was already on his third cup of coffee. "Running is a great way to see the countryside in Greece. When you run, everything is perfect." I didn't expect to hear something so profound at six o'clock on a Sunday morning in a taxicab in Rosemont, Illinois, but there it was. *When you run, everything is perfect.* On that day, in that cab, a random taxicab driver from Greece said something that I'll remember for the rest of my life. I share his words every time I speak publicly about running.

If you were to ask Jon Little, the Olympic Trials running law student, who woke himself up every day with a roll out of bed and onto the hardwood floor, why we run, he would say, "I run because it is one of the only things in life I have found to be truly fair. No amount of money, or political or family connections, can buy fitness or running success. I run because

I enjoy it—I enjoy seeing my body improve, I enjoy listening to my body while I run, I enjoy the soulful feeling I get after a hard effort. I run because I love it."

If you were to ask me why *I* run, as I am often asked, I might say that sounds like a simple question, but it's actually not so simple to answer. I could say I run because it makes me fit. Or I could say I like the challenge of it. Or I could say that I run to prevent the heart attack that my father died of when he was fifty-one years old. All of those reasons are true. But none of them is the right one. I might answer the question by posing one of my own, like my Jewish brethren tend to do: Why does a pianist play the piano? Why does an artist paint? Why does a writer write?

The truth is I've been running for so long that I don't question why I do it. I just do. Six days per week, every week. I don't know how *not* to run. My life can't be any other way. Running is my sustenance. It is my companion, my best friend who is there every day for me to talk to, to lean on, to gain strength from. My mother, who was a widow for twenty-nine years, always said about my father, "He gave me the strength to be me the next day." I suppose that is what running does for me.

Finally, if you were to ask a Zen Master why we run, he might not say anything; he would just start running. Perhaps that's the best answer of them all.

It is impossible to fathom the innumerable factors that can and do motivate a person to run. There is never a single motive that can be isolated as exclusively responsible. We run for a beautiful variety and complexity of reasons, limited only by our ability to understand them. And we run because we can.

HEALTHFUL RUNS

"SHE WAS BECOMING AN EXAMPLE OF NEWTON'S FIRST
LAW OF MOTION—A BODY AT REST STAYS AT REST
UNLESS ACTED ON BY AN OUTSIDE FORCE. I TRIED TO
BE MY MOM'S OUTSIDE FORCE."

In Anchorage, Alaska, twenty-eight-year-old Sabrina Walker heads out the door to run. It's cold outside, as any runner in Alaska would expect it to be, about 20 degrees Fahrenheit on this day. A powdery snow covers the ground. As she takes her first few steps, her breathing is noticeably loud. She has a chronic wet cough, and it sometimes sounds like she's wheezing, as if she has a bad chest cold or pneumonia. It usually takes her about five to ten minutes to catch her breath and find a breathing rhythm that helps her run. People often glance at her, because she sounds very winded. "They probably think I should take a walking break," she jokes.

Despite the coughing and wheezing, she prefers running in colder temperatures rather than hot ones, but if it's colder than 15 degrees outside, she runs indoors at the gym. "I've grown up in Alaska, so the cold is something that I've adjusted to," she says. "Our bodies are very adaptable, and I find my lungs feel so much clearer after a run in the cold." Sabrina often comments on how her lungs feel. Her awareness of them is unlike that of other runners. There have been times when she has coughed up blood after a run.

When Sabrina was four years old and began kindergarten, her parents realized how small she was compared to her classmates. Being one-quarter Tlingit Indian, they took her to the Indian Health Services Hospital in Alaska. Doctors couldn't find anything wrong with her. After months of testing, on the suggestion of a doctor from outside the hospital, she was diagnosed with cystic fibrosis, a life-threatening, genetic lung-and-digestive system disease affecting 30,000 people in the United States and 70,000 people worldwide. Sabrina was born with a defective gene that causes her body to produce unusually thick, sticky mucus that clogs her lungs and leads to life-threatening lung infections. The mucus also obstructs her pancreas and prevents enzymes from breaking down food, which leads to poor absorption of vital nutrients.

Because the cystic fibrosis gene is not carried in the Native American or Alaskan native populations, the Indian Health Services Hospital had never had a patient with cystic fibrosis and had never considered testing her for the disease. The three-quarters of Sabrina that is Caucasian was responsible for her carrying the gene.

Sabrina started running when she was twelve years old. Her father, an elementary school physical-education teacher, always wanted Sabrina to participate in sports. Her mother believed that running could be used as a way to clear her lungs of all that mucus, so she took Sabrina to a local track and set a goal for her to run for ten minutes. She ran with her daughter. "We learned that running helped me to loosen the thick mucus from my lungs and cough it out," Sabrina says. Motivation from her parents led her to compete in middle school and high school cross-country and track-and-field.

When Sabrina was an eighteen-year-old senior in high school, she started to have lower-back pain. Given her age and athletic history of running cross-country and track, her doctor thought that she had pulled a muscle. But the pain didn't go away and eventually got worse. "I started to feel shooting pains down my legs, and my right foot was losing feeling," she remembers.

After graduating from high school desperate for help, she went back to the doctor. This time, the diagnosis was very different: a malignant tumor on her spine. Non-Hodgkin's lymphoma. She underwent a month of radiation and three days of chemotherapy treatment every three weeks for four months. She got pneumonia after her first chemo session, because her body was so weak. She was also allergic to one of the chemotherapy drugs, so it had to be administered very slowly over the course of two days with lots of Benadryl. But it worked. Sabrina has been in remission for nine years. And she still runs in the Alaska cold.

It's Sunday morning. You get out of bed and get ready to go out for a run. The weather is warm. You put on your moisture-wicking socks and shirt, lace your shoes, and head out the door. Before you even take your first step, the cortex of your brain stimulates your autonomic nervous system, which causes your blood vessels to constrict and your blood pressure to rise. Within a few strides of your run, you start to breathe faster and deeper. The number of times your heart beats each minute and the volume of blood your heart ejects with each of those beats both rise to match the greater demand of your muscles for oxygen. More blood flows through your vessels—fifteen to twenty times more than when you're sitting on your couch.

Running occurs from the inside out. To get to the nitty-gritty of how and why running makes us better runners—or makes us runners at all—we have to look inward, inside the black box of our bodies that is slowly becoming a lighter shade of gray with new molecular research. Exercise physiology being a fairly new branch of science, we are still learning what occurs that makes us better runners and makes us more healthful from running. The changes happen even down to the tiniest of cells, where the business of life occurs, and the nucleic acids and bases that make up the helical strands of our DNA. With Nirenberg and Matthaei cracking the first codon of the genetic code in 1961, and the Human Genome Project giving us the entire DNA code in 2003, we can now see inside of us like we have never seen before.

Your literal inner runner is adapting to every running stride you take by making specific changes, so it can handle more work. Running presents small threats to our bodies' survival, and while we're recovering after our runs, our bodies make specific adjustments to assuage the threats. Big changes occur as a result of repeated runs and repeated threats, which lead to a concerted accumulation of structural and functional proteins inside of us that make us fitter, and look and perform better.

One of the first changes is an increase in the volume of blood in your body. Having more blood flowing through your body enhances your blood vessels' capacity to transport oxygen. But that alone is not enough.

Running creates a large spiderweb of tiny capillaries around your muscle fibers, increasing the diffusion of oxygen into the muscles. The more elaborate the spiderweb, the shorter the distance that oxygen must travel to get from a capillary to deep inside the muscle fiber. As the blood gets closer to your muscles through the capillaries, precious oxygen lets go of its tight bind on the hemoglobin protein inside your red blood cells that have been carrying it through the blood vessels, so it can be given up to your muscles.

Not long after you started today's run, your heart rate settles around 140 beats per minute, more than double what it was when you were lying in your bed before you got out the door. The amount of blood returning to your heart through your veins increases to match the amount being sent by the heart through your arteries.

Running is about getting to the heart of the matter. Literally. Perhaps the most elegant adaptation your body makes is an increase in the size of your heart—specifically, the left ventricle, which is responsible for sending blood to everywhere in your body except your lungs. This enlargement of your left ventricle, called left ventricular hypertrophy, results in a greater stroke volume—the volume of blood your heart pumps out with each beat. The larger your left ventricle, the more blood it can hold; the more blood it can hold, the more blood it can pump to the muscles you use to run. In many respects, your ability to become a better runner is dictated by your heart's ability to pump blood and oxygen. Make a better heart, and you make a better runner.

To maintain your running pace on today's run, many enzymes are busy at work in your calves, hamstrings, quadriceps, and other muscles, catalyzing numerous chemical reactions to break down carbohydrates and fat for fuel, including the one that breaks the strong bonds of ATP molecules we learned about in high-school biology class to liberate energy for muscle contraction. Many of those enzymes live inside the mitochondria—the cells' oxygen-using factories—which are responsible for everything inside of us that is aerobic, and that's pretty much everything.

Running is a potent stimulus to proliferate mitochondria. Having more mitochondria in our muscles—along with the enzymes inside of them—increases our muscles' ability to produce energy aerobically, shifting metabolism toward a greater reliance on fat when running at a specific pace. By increasing our muscles' aerobic capacity, we delay their reliance on anaerobic metabolism—chemical reactions that don't use oxygen to produce energy—and thus can run at a faster pace before we begin to fatigue.

The link between an increase in enzyme activity and an increase in mitochondria's capacity to consume oxygen, first discovered in 1967 in the muscles of rats, has provided much insight into the adaptability of skeletal muscle. Generally, the greater the demand, the greater the adaptations—run more miles, make more mitochondria.

While packing our muscles with more mitochondria enables us to hold a faster pace, it also has implications for a broader range of health issues. It is of great interest to scientists, especially because mitochondria are unique in that they have their own DNA. The mitochondria you stimulate your body to make during today's run have particular relevance for our understanding of mitochondrial diseases, the muscle damage induced by free radicals, and the age-related loss of muscle mass known as sarcopenia. If you want healthy, functioning muscles as you age, you need lots of healthy mitochondria. One more reason to run.

Deeper into today's run, all those chemical reactions taking place produce a lot of heat, and the repeated muscle contractions with each running stride cause your body temperature to rise. Since your primary mechanism of cooling your body is through the evaporation of sweat from the surface of your skin, you begin to sweat more. As a result, you lose body water and begin to become dehydrated. Despite all the attention running pays to your muscles, water, not muscle, is the major component of your body. So when you lose water, there are consequences. A major consequence of dehydration is an increase in body temperature when you run. In an attempt to prevent body temperature from rising to dangerous levels, your central nervous system orchestrates a complex response in which blood vessels supplying your organs constrict, while blood vessels supplying your skin dilate, causing blood to be diverted away from your organs and directed outward to increase cooling through the convection of air over your skin's surface. As a result of convective cooling, your skin temperature decreases.

Feeling a bit frisky, you decide to pick up the pace. You start to breathe heavier. Heart rate rises. Blood flow to your muscles increases.

Running changes our muscles, those finely tuned motors of our movements. Analyzing muscle is the most accessible way we have to see what running does to our bodies. However, despite how many compliments you get from your post-run Instagram pictures, what matters is not what your muscles look like, but what they can do.

For years, muscles got a bad rap, serving as a metaphor for the failure of intelligence—the dumb jock. If you had muscles and knew how to use them, it must have meant you didn't have a brain. But things have changed. Muscle has become the poster child of strength, health, and vitality. Muscle is the new sexy.

In the early days, it was the strength of a muscle that garnered all of the attention in the field of physical education. Tests of muscular strength have existed since at least the time of the ancient Olympics, when athletes were required to lift a ball of iron in order to qualify. In 1873, Dr. Dudley Sargent, a pioneer in physical education, initiated strength testing at Harvard University. It has since become an important tool in evaluating muscle characteristics. But muscle can do more than just make us strong; it can also make us endure. And running improves endurance.

Running affects our muscles on a cellular level. Like a fickle homeowner who can't decide if the kitchen should be modeled in English country or art deco, running constantly remodels the contraction mechanics of individual muscle fibers, increasing their diameter and speed of contraction to optimize their function.

Running also stimulates the storage of carbohydrates in your muscles, providing them with more of their preferred choice of fuel. While the public would love to burn more fat on runs, muscles actually prefer to use carbohydrates, because it's a much more efficient fuel to burn. Muscle biopsy research in the 1960s revealed that the ability to perform prolonged endurance exercise is strongly influenced by the amount of carbohydrates our muscles store, with fatigue coinciding with the depletion of those carbohydrates—one of the primary factors responsible for the infamous marathon wall. Like your car's gas tank, our muscles have a limited supply of carbohydrates, perhaps enough for a little more than two hours of running at a moderate pace. When we run more miles and go on longer runs, we teach our muscles to rely on fat as a fuel in an effort to spare the limited carbohydrates for times or speeds that we really need it.

You pick up the pace even more now, huffing and puffing like you're going to blow Grandma's house down. Running fast feels good and comes with its own set of internal changes. It enhances your muscles' unique ability to produce energy without using oxygen by increasing the number of enzymes that catalyze the chemical reactions in our non-oxygen-using pathways.

After a few minutes of fast-paced running, hydrogen starts to accumulate in your muscles from the increased metabolic rate, which makes your muscles more acidic. Like factory workers in a sweatshop inhibited by the heat, this acidity inhibits the work of those enzymes responsible for the chemical reactions inside your muscles. But hydrogen is not the lone culprit here. Other metabolites, including potassium and phosphate, call out "my bad," as they also accumulate in your muscles as you run faster. Together, all of these metabolites, in very specific ways, decrease the force your muscles generate, and your pace slows down. Over time, the faster running increases your muscles' ability to buffer the acidity that develops from the accumulation of hydrogen. Creating a stronger buffer delays fatigue at a given pace.

For today, however, you try as hard as you can to dig deep, with one final push to the end of your run. Your central nervous system sends more frequent signals to recruit your muscle fibers, including the powerful fast-twitch fibers, innervated with their large neurons, to compensate for the fatiguing slow-twitch muscle fibers, which have been working for a while. It worked. You maintain your pace until you get back home.

Collectively, all these changes make us faster runners and improve our health. After many weeks and months and years of running, we see a faster time on the stopwatch at the end of a 5K. We see high cholesterol and blood pressure return to healthy values. We see less fat around our waistlines. We see defined calves.

How we induce these changes is a matter of physiological economics—supply and demand. Evolution has given humans an exceptional ability to adapt. Your body's structure and function match the demands you place on it. If you increase the demand, you increase the amount of change that takes place to keep pace with the increased demand. It's just like the real estate business—the more people who want to move to a specific town, the more houses and apartment buildings are built in that town to accommodate the people moving there. Los Angeles has more housing than Los Alamos, because the demand for places to live is greater in Los Angeles. Running creates a strong demand, and as a result, it creates the forum for change.

At the Lawrence Berkeley National Laboratory on the campus of the University of California–Berkeley, there is a researcher named Paul Williams, PhD, who has devoted much of his career to the study of the effects of running on health. He is the lead researcher of the National Runners' and Walkers' Health Studies, the world's largest and longest-running series of studies on the health benefits of running and walking, which include the tracking of 160,000 participants. Williams and his colleagues have examined the effect of running and walking on everything from obesity to cataracts. And what they have found is astonishing. For every characteristic of a person's health that he and his colleagues have studied, the more people ran, the better the outcome or the lower the disease risk.

In one of the studies, 41,582 female runners were divided into groups based on their age and the number of miles they ran per week. Compared with those who ran less than 10 miles per week, those who averaged over 40 miles per week had 10 percent lower body mass index (your weight divided by your squared height, the most common value used to determine obesity), 8 percent lower waist circumference, 7 percent lower hip circumference, and 4 percent lower chest circumference. In every age group, the greater the number of miles run per week, the lower the body mass index and chest, waist, and hip circumferences.

Of course, cross-sectional research like this cannot determine cause and effect, since it is possible that smaller people with lower body mass indices may run more, because they have bodies more suitable for running. However, the very large sample size increases the statistical power of the study, making it more likely that the statistical differences are indeed due to the experimental treatment.

To get around the limitations of cross-sectional studies, in another study the researchers followed 29,139 men and 11,985 women for seven and a half years to examine the relationship between cardiorespiratory fitness (as measured by 10-kilometer running performance), weekly running distance, and the incidence of high blood pressure, high cholesterol, and diabetes. At the end of the study, they found that 8.53 percent of the men and 4.26 percent of the women developed high blood pressure, 12.2 percent of the men and 5.14 percent of the women developed high cholesterol, and 0.68 percent of the men and 0.23 percent of the women became diabetic. Interestingly, running more miles per week predicted a lower incidence of high blood pressure, high cholesterol, and diabetes in both men and women. Specifically, the odds for developing high cholesterol significantly decreased with each 10-mile-per-week increment in distance through 40 miles per week for men and 30 miles per week for women. The health benefits of running continued to accrue through at least 40 miles per week.

A person's cardiorespiratory fitness also influenced his or her health. The scientists found that the faster people ran for 10 kilometers, the lower their odds for developing high blood pressure and cholesterol. Specifically, men's odds for developing high blood pressure and cholesterol declined linearly with faster 10-kilometer race times through a time of 39:07.

Compared to the least-fit men, the fittest men (those who ran faster than 44:20 for 10 kilometers) had 62 percent lower odds for developing high blood pressure, 67 percent lower odds for developing high cholesterol, and 86 percent lower odds for becoming diabetic. The women's odds for developing high cholesterol also declined significantly with faster 10-kilometer race times through a time of 41:34. Compared to the least-fit women, women who ran faster than 51:57 for 10 kilometers had significantly lower odds for developing high blood pressure. The obvious conclusion that can be drawn here is that the faster you can run, at least up to a point, the better your cardiometabolic health.

For people at risk of diabetes—characterized by the insufficient use of glucose from either a lack of insulin or cells that don't respond to insulin—running makes cells more sensitive and responsive to insulin, which increases muscles' uptake of glucose. Running also increases the activity of the proteins that transport glucose from the blood into cells.

In yet another study from the National Runners' and Walkers' Health Studies series, researchers charted the running habits and body weight of 3,973 men and 1,444 women who quit running, 270 men and 146 women who started running, and 420 men and 153 women who remained sedentary during seven and a half years. They found that body weight and intra-abdominal fat decreased in the people who started running and increased in the people who stopped running, with the changes proportional to the change in the amount they ran. In other words, the more the previously sedentary people ran, the greater the decrease in body weight and intra-abdominal fat. Conversely, the more the runners backed off on how much they ran, the more their body weight and intra-abdominal fat increased. Any runner who has ever been injured and can't run knows how easy it is to put on weight. Running is one of the best ways to keep the weight off.

Another interesting type of study to consider is one conducted on twins. Studying identical twins is a clever way to examine the health effects of exercise, because researchers can control for the large, confounding variable of genetics. Being a twin myself, I always love reading twin studies. My twin brother and I are fraternal, which means we share only half of our DNA (two sperm fertilized two eggs at the same time). Identical twins are just that—they have identical DNA (one sperm fertilized one egg, and the egg split in half). So, studying identical twins enables scientists to isolate the effects of environment or a given treatment—in this case, running—on a specific outcome, such as health. If one identical twin runs and the other doesn't, what will the difference in their health be?

Williams and his colleagues examined thirty-five pairs of identical twins who differed in their exercise behavior. In each pair, one twin was a runner while the other was not. The "running" twins ran an average of 39 miles per week, while the mostly sedentary twins averaged just four miles per week. Compared to the sedentary twins, the running twins had significantly lower body mass index and significantly higher values of high-density lipoprotein (HDL, often referred to as the "good" cholesterol) and its major protein component, apolipoprotein A-1, particularly among males. HDL is a protein that acts as a scavenger of cholesterol, triglycerides, and other fats, removing them from blood vessels and transporting them to the liver, where they get disposed. The higher your HDL value, the lower your risk for cardiovascular disease. It's been known for a long time that aerobic exercise increases the concentration of HDL in the blood.

One of the main conclusions from this series of studies is that more running is better than less running, and faster running is better than slower running. There are a number of studies to show that body weight is directly proportional to the amount and intensity of exercise. Running is closely linked to body weight.

It was a typical hazy, hot, and humid day in central New Jersey when my plane landed at Newark Airport on September 1, 2010. Every time I travel across the country to visit my family from where I live in San Diego, I make sure I get my run done early in the morning before I leave. There's hardly a place I can go where the weather is as good as it is in San Diego, and I need the strength from running to deal with my family. Most families have a unique dynamic, and mine, as small as it is, has one of its own. Running is the "deep breath" I take before visiting my family. I'm lucky that my family is close and perhaps less dysfunctional than most. But this time, I would need as deep a breath as my lungs could hold.

When I arrived in Newark, I hopped on a New Jersey Transit bus to take me to see my mother. At seventy-five, she was in an assisted-living residence. The bus dropped me off at the station, and I walked the mile to the assisted-living residence. I spotted my mom's blue Buick parked in the lot. A film of dirt created a screen on the windshield. Leaves collected in the gutter between the windshield and the hood. I knew the car hadn't been driven for a while. I opened the door with my spare key and drove to the hospital, where she had been admitted earlier that day. As I approached a stoplight, I pushed the brake pedal all the way to the floor of the car for it to come to a stop. It needed new brakes thousands of miles ago.

My mom was suffering from bone cancer, which had metastasized from the breast cancer that had been diagnosed twelve years earlier. Before leaving for New Jersey, I spoke to my twin brother, who lives in New York.

"What happened? I asked.

My mom was hospitalized because of jaundice—her skin and the whites of her eyes had turned yellow, which occurs because of failure of the liver to metabolize a protein called bilirubin, the yellow product that results from the breakdown of iron. When bilirubin can't be processed by the liver, it accumulates in the blood and the space outside of cells, causing a yellowing of the skin and eyes. She wasn't doing well.

The doctor placed a stent in her liver duct to open it. It worked. In a couple of days, the jaundice was gone. She seemed to be doing better. But she was still in a lot of pain. She hadn't been moving much ever since her femur broke three years earlier from a fall in her bedroom when she lived alone in her house. Every time I'd visit, I tried to get her to exercise from her wheelchair, so she could strengthen her leg. She was afraid she'd fall again if she stood up to walk. She was becoming an example of Newton's first law of motion—a body at rest stays at rest unless acted on by an outside force. I tried to be my mom's outside force.

The next two weeks were the most difficult time of my life. I ran most mornings before going to the hospital. Sometimes, I ran in the dark at night after leaving. My deep breath.

Lying in the hospital bed, my mom was even more sedentary than she was before. She was in almost-constant back pain. She developed blood clots in both of her legs that prompted placement of a Greenfield filter at the lower end of the vena cava to prevent the clots from traveling to her heart and lungs. It seemed we were heading down a slippery slope.

I spent two weeks in the hospital with my mom, my twin brother and I sitting by her side and holding her hands until all was literally said and done. It was the most emotional experience I've ever had.

My mom was a tough physical-education teacher from the Bronx. She taught kids with guns and kids from mafia families. She had an admirable strength, competing in the Roller Derby as a member of the New York Chiefs. She skydived. She played semi-pro softball with her iconic four-fingered glove (she had five fingers like everyone else, but baseball gloves in those days had only four). She raised twin sons as a single mother after our father passed away when we were eight years old. And she cared for her own elderly mother, who was her best friend. She worried about me every day I walked out the door to run. She came to every one of my middle-school and high-school races and even every race I ran in the area when I visited her as an adult. She had a personality that you thought could never die. So when I made the trip from San Diego to New Jersey two weeks earlier, I never thought I would be planning a funeral. I didn't pack a suit.

Every day over the final two weeks of my mother's life, I ran to find myself and to gain the strength that I needed to be there for her. And for myself. Running can give us an enormous amount of strength. Emotional stress has physical consequences. Most everyone has experienced the physical symptoms that stress or anxiety causes. So when my mother was in the hospital, every day I ran I wasn't thinking about running the way I usually do—as a way to train for my next race. Instead, I used running to strengthen myself, to steel myself from the stress. Years later, I often go for a run when I think about my mother, as a way to deal with the sadness and the emotions and prevent them from becoming overwhelming.

During my runs in the days and weeks following her death, I thought about how lonely and isolated an experience dying is. No matter how many people are by your side, it is a singular, individual moment, a stark contrast to the plurality of daily living. As your soul escapes from your flesh, no one can feel what you feel. I don't know how much or even the nature of the pain my mom felt, or the exact moment at which my mom didn't feel death anymore, the moment when her central nervous system shut down from the lack of oxygen. If I get nothing else from my running, I hope that it will help me deal with that experience when it is my turn.

Running is closely linked to our state of mind. Most runners would agree that running lifts their spirits. Many runners go out for a run when they feel sad or depressed. They come back rejuvenated. If you want a great way to exchange a bad mood for a good one, go for a run. Turns out that this is not just anecdotal. Research has shown that aerobic exercise, running being the most often-studied type, is just as effective as prescription drugs for ameliorating depression and making you feel good.

Take, for example, a 1999-collaborative study from scientists at Duke University, the University of Colorado–Boulder, and the University of California–San Diego, which was published in the scientific journal *Archives of Internal Medicine*. The researchers randomly divided 156 men and women, aged fifty years and older, who were diagnosed with major depressive disorder into three groups: one group did aerobic exercise, one group took an antidepressant medication, and the third group combined exercise with the antidepressant medication. The subjects were evaluated for depression using standardized tests and criteria, before and after the treatments. The exercise consisted of three supervised sessions per week for sixteen weeks, during which the subjects warmed up for ten minutes, then walked or ran for thirty minutes at 70 to 85 percent of their heart-rate reserve, followed by a five-minute cooldown. After sixteen weeks, all three groups exhibited significant and comparable declines in clinical symptoms of depression. There was no difference in the depression test scores between those in the antidepressant medication group, exercise group, and combined medication-and-exercise group. Other studies have found the same results.

One reason running decreases symptoms of depression is that—like antidepressant medications and recreational, addictive drugs—running increases serotonin, a neurotransmitter (a type of chemical that relays signals from one area of the brain to another) responsible for feelings of well-being and happiness.

Serotonin is a powerful neurotransmitter, directly or indirectly influencing most of your approximately 40,000,000 brain cells. A number of studies have shown increases in serotonin levels or in its precursor, tryptophan, following exercise.

Dr. David Nieman is one of the world's leading authorities on exercise and immune function. His research, and that of others, has elucidated an interesting relationship between exercise and our chances of getting sick. Both a single run and chronic running alter the number and function of circulating immune-system cells, including neutrophils, monocytes, and natural killer cells. Moderate amounts of running increase these cells and strengthen your immune system, reducing your risk of developing a cold or any other type of upper respiratory tract infection. However, periods of intense or prolonged training or racing, most notably marathon or ultramarathon running, decrease the circulating levels of these cells and weaken your immune system, increasing the risk for an upper respiratory tract infection.

Dr. Nieman's research has shown that runners training more than 60 miles per week double their odds for sickness compared to those training fewer than 20 miles per week. That's because many components of the immune system exhibit change after prolonged, heavy exercise, leaving a window open to infection. If you've ever trained for a marathon, you may have gotten sick soon after completing the race. This is quite common, because the marathon stresses the immune system extensively, with a major increase in pro-inflammatory markers. It seems that the functioning of the immune system is one of the few cases in which more running is not better than some running, but some running is definitely better than not running at all.

As part of a recent routine physical, I got some blood work done and tested positive for a homozygous mutation of the methylenetetrahydrofolate reductase (MTHFR) gene, which encodes the enzyme of the same name. MTHFR is a key enzyme in the metabolism of folate, which is involved in the production of red blood cells. A homozygous mutation means that both copies of the gene have the mutation, and may have medical implications, like an increased risk for vascular disease. A heterozygous mutation—only one copy of the gene has the mutation while the other does not—is considered medically insignificant. My father died of a heart attack when he was fifty-one years old, both of my grandfathers died of heart attacks before I was born, and my mother and maternal grandmother had pacemakers. Given the heart disease on both sides of my family, it wasn't too big a surprise to find out that I have a possible genetic marker for vascular or heart disease.

As a lifelong runner, I've spent a lot of time wondering if it's possible to outrun bad genes. Will I die of a heart attack like my father, or will running protect me from that fate? Runner and author Jim Fixx, whose 1977 book, *The Complete Book of Running*, became a national bestseller, may have been the first runner to bring national attention to running and health. When he died on the street during a run at age fifty-two, it made national news, and people, even doctors, started saying that running is bad for one's health. In 2007, at the US Olympic Marathon Trials in New York, twenty-eight-year-old elite runner Ryan Shay collapsed and died five and a half miles into the race. But both Fixx and Shay had underlying heart problems. Running did not cause their deaths. Fixx was a pack-a-day, overweight smoker, who ate cheeseburgers until he started running at age thirty-five, and his father had a heart attack at age thirty-five and died of another one at forty-three. At the time of his death, Fixx was still eating cheeseburgers (he was adamant in his belief that running protected against poor nutrition) and had atherosclerosis, with one coronary artery blocked 95 percent, a second artery blocked 85 percent, and a third blocked 70 percent. Shay had a cardiac arrhythmia due to an enlarged heart that was diagnosed years earlier.

No matter how much we run, our health is still heavily influenced by our genotype—the genetic makeup of our microscopic cells that lie deep within us and provide the code for who we are. But running can alter the way those genes express themselves and interact with our environment—our phenotype—to create our observable traits. And that's where running holds its greatest power.

Turns out that running has the remarkable ability to change our phenotype and even the way we use our genetic code. We can't change the genes we were given from our parents, so if you've maxed out your training, and you're still not an elite or sub-elite runner, no amount of training, no matter how intelligently planned it may be, is going to change that. But genes are constantly being activated and inhibited—turned on and off—depending on the biochemical signals they receive from their environment. And exercise, especially when that exercise is repeated over and over and over again, such that it becomes a chronic state for the organism, is one of the best environments for causing change. We have certain genes that become active or dormant with exercise. For example, when we run, a process called methylation chemically modifies our muscles' DNA to give us more energy through their metabolic pathways. DNA methylation occurs in our blood, skeletal muscle, cardiac muscle, adipose tissue, and even our brain. When DNA is methylated, genes become more responsive to signals in their environment, which regulates protein function and overall health. For example, DNA methylation in skeletal muscle and adipose tissue directly influences lipogenesis—the formation and subsequent storage of body fat. That's why running is so good for reducing body fat. Running significantly decreases markers of lipogenesis while increasing markers of lipolysis—the opposite process that breaks down fat for subsequent metabolism. Scientists from Lund University in Sweden have identified 134 individual genes that changed in the degree of DNA methylation after six months of aerobic exercise for three hours per week, consisting of one one-hour spinning class and two one-hour aerobics classes.

In another study, scientists at the highly regarded Karolinska Institute in Stockholm, Sweden, had twenty-three young and healthy men and women undergo a series of physical and medical tests, including a muscle biopsy, and then had them cycle on a stationary bicycle in the lab at a moderate pace for forty-five minutes, four times per week for three months. However, they included a unique twist in their study—the subjects cycled with only one leg while the other leg did nothing, so the researchers could isolate the effect of the exercise on the subjects' genes. After three months, the subjects repeated the muscle biopsies and other tests.

Not surprisingly, the subjects' exercised leg was more powerful than the other, showing that the exercise had resulted in physical improvements. But the DNA between legs was also different. Using sophisticated genomic analysis, the researchers discovered that more than 5,000 sites on the genome of muscle cells from the exercised leg showed significant changes in DNA methylation and gene expression, while the DNA of the unexercised leg remained unchanged. Most of the examined genes play a role in energy metabolism, insulin response, and muscle inflammation. It seems that not only does exercise make us healthier, it does so on a genomic level.

A couple of months after finding out that I have a homozygous mutation of the MTHFR gene, I raced a mile in a track meet, and I strained my calf muscle. It's happened before while running fast intervals on the track, so while it was concerning, I didn't think much of it. I'd been getting some calf strains lately with speed work, and I thought that perhaps my age was affecting my calf muscles' ability to keep up with my zeal for intense training and racing. Later that night, I started having severe chest pains. I couldn't sleep, because it hurt too much to lie down. The pain even prevented me from taking deep breaths. If I didn't have reason to believe it was something else, I would have thought I was having a heart attack. But I had reason to believe it was something else, because I've had this pain before, a couple of months after a bout of pneumonia. Last time, I found out that the pain was caused by pleuritis— inflammation of the lining of the lungs. A CT angiogram—a fancy x-ray with an intravenous iodine injection that acts as a dye to highlight the lungs' vasculature—revealed a pulmonary embolism. I had a tiny blood clot in my right lung.

Now, over two years later, with another episode of the same pain, I had a feeling I knew what it was. Another CT angiogram revealed three pulmonary emboli, and an ultrasound of my legs revealed a few deep vein thromboses in my calves. Clots sometimes develop in the large calf veins when blood pools in the legs, and those clots can travel through the venous circulation to the lungs. To get to the lungs, the clot must travel through the right atrium and right ventricle of the heart. If the clot is large enough, it can get stuck in the heart, block blood flow, and cause a heart attack. If it passes through the heart into the lungs, it can be life threatening if it is large enough to occlude a major vessel.

Luckily, the clots I had were small enough not to cause an immediate threat to my life. I was put on anticoagulant to prevent more clots. Over time, my veins will re-canalize—form new vessels for blood flow around the obstructed clot sites. The body is very smart that way. When red blood cells run into traffic, your body's construction workers create an alternate route.

Other than that mutation of the MTHFR gene, blood tests haven't yet revealed that I have any genetic markers that predispose my blood to clotting, so I'm not sure what caused it. I haven't been on any long, international flights lately, and although I do sit at a desk a lot, I take breaks to walk around and try to drink enough water to stay hydrated. What happens inside of us is often a mystery.

When I got the diagnosis of the blood clots, my first thought was, "Am I going to die?" And then, immediately following that first thought, came another: "Will I be able to run again?"

How peculiar. At a time when I felt vulnerable and wondered if something were going to happen to me, why would I wonder if I could run? It has taken me thirty-one years of running to be able to begin answering that question, and I'm still learning the answer. Running is so much a part of my identity of being human that I cannot imagine my life without it.

It is both a great asset and a great tragedy to have something so meaningful and profound in one's life. I'm not sure many people have something like that. Running and coaching have been deeply fulfilling endeavors for me. But if running is so important to me and my definition of myself, what am I to do if something were to take it away? Would I be able to continue living a meaningful life? The thing that scares me the most is that I don't know the complete answer to that question.

I've been very lucky to have never had a major running-related injury or illness that has kept me away from running for very long. I've had only four instances in my life that prevented me from running for more than a week—two fractured bones (from doing things other than running), a bout of pneumonia, and blood clots in my lungs. There have been only a few other times that I have had to back off on my training or take a day or two off because of something minor—a chest cold, Achilles tendonitis, a strained calf muscle, and bruised ribs from falling on the cement during a run in the rain.

It's an understatement to say that runners hate to be injured or sick. It affects our lives in innumerable ways, none of which seem positive at the time it's happening. Indeed, I have never met any other type of athlete or fitness buff, recreational or elite, who hates being injured more than runners. For better or for worse, from the time I first started running and racing as an eleven-year-old kid, my identity has been linked to being a runner. Running makes me feel powerful and fit. I feel like an athlete. When I'm fit, really fit, I walk with a swagger and my head held high and full of confidence. Life seems full of possibilities. When something happens that prevents me from running, even for one day that wasn't planned as a rest day, that identity is taken away. When that one day turns into a week or more, I get antsy, irritable, guilty, and, yes, I even feel fat and out of shape. When what's preventing me from running is health related, I feel vulnerable, scared, weak. I feel like the illness has taken away all of my power and vibrancy. It may sound silly and irrational, but I feel like something is wrong with my life if I can't run. Things just don't feel right. I've been taken out of the community of runners, races passing me by like a train I was supposed to be on. Social media makes it worse. I see friends and running acquaintances posting photos of their runs on Facebook and Instagram, tweeting about their races on Twitter, while I sit at home missing out on the action. I'm not the same person when I don't run. And everything else suffers. I sometimes even start to experience phantom pains in other parts of my body. All of a sudden, I feel a twinge in my calf or an itch in my hamstring. Luckily, this kind of thing doesn't happen very often, because I'm one of those non-injured runners. But it's happened enough that I know I don't ever want it to happen again. Like the idle Porsche that doesn't like to sit on the driveway, my body feels like it has to run to run right. Why buy a Porsche if you're not going to drive it?

Interestingly, I never see this attitude with other types of athletes or others who work out a lot. I know a lot of people in the fitness industry—personal trainers, group exercise instructors, exercise DVD stars—and none of them get all ornery if they miss their workouts for a couple of days. But with runners, there's a sense of impending doom if they can't run.

Beginning in the seventh grade, I became fascinated with time, specifically how fast it moves and how each year seems to go faster than the previous one. As runners, our perception of time is often a bit quirky. The second half of a run always seems to go faster than the first half, and some runs seem to fly by, while others drag on. This changing perception of time may be partly explained by its relationship to effort, as running philosopher Dr. George Sheehan once noted: "The faster we run, the longer it takes." When we are injured or sick, and can't run, our perception of time also changes, as it seems like it takes forever to get back outside, running. But taking a few weeks or months off from running is really only a small blip on the radar when compared to the many years of running that make up our running lives.

Tara Ricciuto was an all-state runner in high school and ran at a couple of NCAA Division I colleges on scholarship. She was talented and never timid about doing the training. But throughout high school and college, she was often injured with stress fractures. Every time she was diagnosed with another stress fracture, she would cross-train in the gym like she was training for the Cross-Fit Olympics (before Cross-Fit even existed), doing interval workouts on the stationary bike, running in the pool, even trying to run on land.

"I worked hard cross-training, so I could be as fit as possible, because the competition was intense in Division I track and cross-country," she says. "In college, I just wanted to be healthy and be able to race to my ability. I felt like there was a really small window of time to accomplish what I wanted to do. I thought I wouldn't even run after college, so it was important to me that I accomplished what I wanted to while still in college. I also was trying to live up to my coaches' expectations and the potential that they believed I had."

She was so driven that she never let her injuries heal, so she kept getting injured over and over again. Between her numerous injuries, she had periods of running brilliance. I admired her tenacity and her will to be a great runner. Unfortunately, she often took it too far and never became the level of runner she could have been if she were able to train consistently for a few years without interruption due to injuries. During one of her injured periods, I took a road trip with Tara to the Penn Relays track meet in Philadelphia to watch the rest of her team run, and she nearly bit my head off, because I didn't make plans to find a gym in the city for her to do her workout.

When we lose our ability to run because of illness or injury, it's easy to feel helpless, vulnerable, and even scared, because the fitness and vibrancy we get from running is taken away. With all the people who don't want to exercise, it's a sealed box to be in when you're entirely willing but physically unable to or precluded from running. There is a huge difference between not wanting it and having it taken away.

My biggest disappointment that comes from not running, and from the accompanying loss of fitness, is the existential crises and near-depression that mounts. I've always seen myself as someone working on being the complete package of a sound mind in a sound body. Running is a huge part of me, but I struggle with it not being all of me. On days that I don't run, which are few and far between, I feel guilty, like I missed out on something important. I suppose this falls within the realm of addiction, and I guess others would say I'm addicted to running. Interestingly, research has shown that the risk for exercise addiction is associated with narcissism. Highly committed exercisers have substantially higher levels of narcissism than less committed exercisers. Am I so narcissistic that I can't miss a single run?

When I can't run, I am soundly disappointed to find such weakness and doubt. Surely I cannot be so lame that the only thing that matters is chasing a time on the stopwatch or looking good in the mirror. I have so many other things to be happy about and thankful for, but here I am feeling weak, out of shape, under-engaged, and anxious.

When I can't run, I feel an even greater, more intense desire to help others achieve their goals. I have loved coaching for a long time, but when illness or injury prevents me from running, I find that I am even more passionate about helping other runners. At those times, I can't direct the energy toward my own running, so I want to direct it toward someone who can run—much like a parent who lives vicariously through his or her talented child.

It's hard to say that my few injuries or other illness-driven breaks from running were ever worth it as a learning experience, because, quite frankly, it sucks and I want to run. What do injuries teach you anyway? That you can't do what you want to do in the way you want to do it? If you get injured while training for a marathon, does that teach you that you can't run a marathon? That's not what you want to learn.

Perhaps injuries teach you the importance of training smarter. But you don't necessarily need an injury to learn that lesson. I've spent my entire career trying to teach runners and coaches how to train intelligently, and I've written multiple books about it. If nothing else, injuries or other forced times off certainly do encourage you to put things in perspective. Each time I return to running, I am more thankful for it and feel a growing sense that I must take care that my life would still be fulfilling if I were never able to run again. Not running doesn't detract from my value as a person, nor does it yours, although it often may feel like it does. We are more than a weekly mileage total or a PR. We are more than a VO_2max value or a 10-mile run or a bib number. Yet we are all of those things, too. Running does not define who we are; *we* define who we are.

Runners get injured. It sucks, and we want nothing more than to get back on the road or the track and run again. But to live the life of a runner, you must let injuries heal rather than try to train through them like my friend Tara did. When you're injured, try to discern the cause of the injury and do whatever you can to prevent it from recurring. While you're recovering, do only those activities that don't worsen the injury or slow the healing process. All training begins with a base of health. Always listen to your body.

I have a friend who thinks I have some philosophical aversion to strength training. As a hardcore weight lifter and successful group fitness instructor who has created many workout DVDs, she tells me that I'm unbalanced, because all I do is run. Although I do choose to run as my daily workout, I keep promising her that I will one day incorporate some upper-body strength training to make my biceps as big as my calves. The truth is I have no aversion, philosophical or otherwise, to strength training. It just doesn't provide the same satisfaction for me as running.

Arguably, cardiovascular exercise will always be more important than strength training throughout your life, because heart disease is the most common cause of death for both men and women. No one has ever died of a weak bicep muscle. However, strength training is still important and becomes more important as people age. I'd even go as far to say that every person over the age of fifty should strength train, because that's about the age at which people start to lose a significant amount of muscle mass. And that loss in muscle mass with age—called sarcopenia—affects your ability to function. If you've ever seen a senior citizen try to stand up from sitting in a chair or witnessed how catastrophic a fall can be to a senior, you know how much benefit strength training can have. The positive effects of strength training on bone density, muscular strength and endurance, balance and coordination, functional mobility, physical aesthetics, and self-esteem cannot be denied.

But even given the ability of strength training to do all that, and give me biceps and shoulders that would make women swoon, I still opt for a running workout over the dumbbells. And I know many other runners who do the same. Most runners would gladly exchange shapely biceps for the PRs of the wispy-thin Kenyans and Ethiopians. Most runners would agree that no other activity can take the place of running. That feeling—that no other activity can take the place of running—is distinct to runners. If an ideal form of exercise exists, runners already know what it is, and they are already doing it. You seldom hear a cyclist say there is no substitute for cycling or a weight lifter say there is no substitute for weight lifting. If an "inner weight lifter" exists, it's hard to imagine it affording the same benefits, the same raison d'être, as the inner runner.

I think perhaps the reason lies in the simplicity of running—it is just you and the freedom of your movement. There is no external equipment. No weights to lift, no bicycle on which to change gears. When you run, your legs are the gears. To run faster or longer, there is nothing to overcome but yourself.

As positive an effect running has on your health, not running has an equally negative effect. A sedentary lifestyle affects your health so much that it's considered one of the seven primary risk factors for heart disease. Lack of physical activity also increases the risk of certain types of cancer. Don't exercise, and you simply have a greater chance of dying. That's a scary thought, because we usually associate poor health with the things we do, like smoking, eating high cholesterol and fatty foods, eating too much sugar and processed foods, drinking alcohol, and using recreational drugs. How many times are we told throughout our lives that smoking causes cancer? Everyone knows that. But we're never told that not exercising causes cancer. We don't usually think about the consequences of *not* doing something. But just as physical activity produces unique cellular signals and physiological responses, so too does inactivity. For example, inactivity quickly engages signals that cause suppression of the enzyme lipoprotein lipase, which contributes to poor fat metabolism, weight gain, and obesity. Conversely, running increases lipoprotein lipase enzyme activity, which enhances fat metabolism. By not exercising, we increase the likelihood of plenty of diseases and maladies, including heart disease, certain types of cancer, diabetes, and even atrophy of our brains. Think about that for a minute. Go ahead, I'll wait. *In the absence of aerobic exercise, we cause illness and disease.* Does running make us live longer? Well, I don't know. It's hard to say that something makes us live longer. Science can't really tell. But there's a good chance that it does.

We always hear about the things we should stop doing or not do. We are told to stop smoking. We are told to stop drinking. We are told to stop eating foods with a high salt content or high-fructose corn syrup or gluten or carbohydrates. The many proponents of low-carb diets would have the public believe that carbohydrates are some kind of poison. Pasta kills us, we are told, so don't eat it. Parents tell their kids don't do this or don't do that.

However, if we *start* something or *do* something that gives us pleasure and fulfills us, we automatically stop doing the things that don't. And the things that cause pain or ill health in our lives start to fade away. We don't need to tell a runner to stop smoking. A smoker will quickly stop smoking by becoming a runner. Running connects us to the things we *should* do to live a healthy life.

There is so much scientific evidence to prove the biological benefits of running that it's fair to say that running may be the single, best thing you can do for your health. It's even more important than eating your vegetables.

Although running carries a slight acute risk of a heart attack by causing an increase in blood pressure, heart rate, and cardiac output, the chronic benefits strongly outweigh the minor acute risk. If you have a very important meeting or event to attend in thirty minutes, and you want to live for the next hour, don't run. The tragedies of Jim Fixx and Ryan Shay remind us of the power of our genes. But if you want to live for the next thirty or forty years, you should run on most days of the week because of the effect that running has on the expression of our genes.

Your inner health—the lining of your blood vessels, the cleanness of your coronary arteries, the levels of glucose and sodium and other nutrients in your blood, the amount of inflammation in your cells—is affected by how much and how hard you run. From reduced blood cholesterol and decreased risk of developing diabetes to the improvement in cognitive function and attenuation of depression, there is no drug, no injection, no other single way you can attain all of the benefits of daily running. If all of the health benefits of running could be harvested into a pill, it would be the most often and widely prescribed drug in the world. We run because our lives depend on it.

It was chilly and breezy on November 3, 2013, as I stood among 50,000 runners from all over the world on the Staten Island side of the Verrazano Narrows Bridge, waiting for the sound of the cannon to start the New York City Marathon. A pink breast-cancer ribbon was pinned to my shirt's left breast to remember my mom, who lost hers to a mastectomy. When the cannon fired, Frank Sinatra, whom my mother skipped school as a kid to see perform, sang "New York, New York" through the speakers, I fist bumped one of the police officers guarding the area, and I looked up to sky and said to my mother, "Here we go."

The 2013 New York City Marathon was my first marathon in twelve years. Even though I've been a lifelong runner, I've stayed away from the marathon, because I am not a marathoner. I've always been better at the shorter, faster races. I love speed. I'd rather put on a pair of spikes and race the mile on the track than run 26.2 miles on the road. I love the feeling of racing in spikes. But there was something that had been calling me ever since my mother passed away in 2010. So twelve years after I ran my first and only marathon, I decided to train for another one and return to where I'm from, where my entire family is from, and run through the streets of New York to raise money for the American Cancer Society in memory of the strongest woman I've ever known. If she could deal with the pain of cancer and the depression and despair that she experienced at end of her life, I could certainly run another marathon. She gave me legs that can run, after all.

For one of the few races of my running life, the New York City Marathon wasn't about the time on the clock. It wasn't even about me. It was about wanting to do something in memory of my mom and my dad, both of whom left this world much too early. And when I ran into the Bronx, the borough where my mom was born and lived until she got married, and when I ran into Brooklyn, the borough where my dad was born and where we lived as a family until my father passed away, I remembered those days, that family, and that life that used to be. For three and a half hours of running, the marathon brought me home.

Among the 50,000 runners who ran the New York City Marathon that year, there are 50,000 stories. At the start line of any major marathon, you'll hear a story from every runner. Some run to save their lives after a heart attack. Some run to prevent one. Some run because they got sick and tired of being overweight. Some run because they made a promise to a dying relative. And some are like me on that cold day in New York: I was running in memory of someone I love, someone who told me when growing up that I can be anyone or do anything I want, someone who encouraged me to pursue my goals, even if it meant living in a different country for a couple of years, someone who told me I'm just as smart as my very smart twin brother.

During the last three years of my mother's life, she couldn't walk without the help of someone else. But she gave me legs and an inner strength that could. I ran because she couldn't.

Running empowers us and strengthens us to do things that we wouldn't or couldn't otherwise do.

Breathing with cystic fibrosis is like breathing through a straw. The airways in the lungs become inflamed and can be blocked from very thick and sticky mucus. Over time, the lungs create scar tissue from fighting infections, rendering parts of the lung unable to function normally. Only 81 percent of Sabrina Walker's lungs function properly.

"I learned to run and cough at the same time—and sometimes pee my shorts in the process—in order to clear my lungs of the mucus building up," she says. "When I clear my lungs, I can get more air in my airways. The effort to rid my lungs of the mucus is a daily task that never ends." Those times she coughs up blood after a run mean that she's fighting an infection and that she worked her lungs too hard.

Running is not just something Sabrina likes to do; it's actually part of her medical routine. It enables her to cough up the thick and sticky mucus that harbors bacteria and causes lung infections. "There is no better way to physically work my lungs like running," she says. "I feel that running keeps my lungs, mind, and body healthy. Running holds me accountable for my own health."

With a degree in elementary education from the University of Colorado–Denver, she had to make a tough decision to set teaching aside, so she wouldn't risk lung infection from being around kids. She married her high-school sweetheart, and after being told that she may be infertile from the chemotherapy, radiation, and cystic fibrosis, she and her husband had their first child in March 2015.

To date, Sabrina has run more than ten half-marathons, three 16-mile mountain trail runs, and many 10Ks and 5Ks. Her next goal is to run a marathon. When asked what running has enabled her to do that she couldn't have done otherwise, she reels off a list of things that would make any healthy runner take a step back and realize just how lucky he or she is.

"Running has let me live life instead of grasp for it. It has helped me to stay active and fit, and has kept me healthy enough to pursue higher education, get married, dream about my future, and conceive and carry a child despite all the odds of not being able to do so. Running has kept me off of the lung transplant list and out of the hospital for the last four years. It has provided me with the opportunity to be hopeful for a cure for cystic fibrosis in my lifetime."

Despite her health issues, Sabrina knows she's lucky, too. "Not everyone has the capability to run," she acknowledges. "Cystic fibrosis and cancer are not excuses to keep me from running; they will continue to fuel the fire that inspires me to run. Running is a way to keep my soul, lungs, and body happy. I have the ability to run, and I will continue to do so until it is not possible. Running keeps me alive."

BETTER RUNS

"THE BEST THINGS IN LIFE CAN COME
FROM UNEXPECTED PLACES."

Owsley County sits in the eastern mountain coalfields of Kentucky. With a population of just 4,755, it is Kentucky's second-smallest county. According to the 2010 census, Owsley County has the second-highest level of child poverty of any county in the United States.

In the small, eighty-one-person town of Booneville, it's senior day for the Owsley County High School Cross Country Team. Cody Johnson and the other seniors are being honored before the final home race of the season.

Cody started running in seventh grade, as a holdback from basketball. Deciding to give cross-country a try, he quickly fell in love with the sport. He had a successful high-school career, winning the regional 800-meter title in track and placing in the top five in every regional competition.

In cases like this, when athletes do well, attention is often given to the coach of the team. But at Cody's school, the coach was not much of a coach at all.

"The coach was very uncaring," Cody says. "We never had a practice of any sort the entire time I was in school."

So Cody did what any seventh grader would do—he trained all by himself, got some advice at cross-country meets from coaches of opposing teams, and read many articles and books to educate himself.

It worked. "I was very successful my first year competing in middle school and earned a spot on the varsity team in eighth grade." Continuing to train on his own, he became the top runner on the team by the end of the season and missed qualifying for the state championships by only five seconds.

"All of that success made me very humble and responsible," he says.

The next year, after completing his freshman year of high school, he ran some local 3K and 5K races over the summer and got some competition from a local runner named Logan Campbell, who was about to start his freshman year at Owsley County High School. But Cody and Logan would not be teammates. They would be rivals, because Cody did not attend Owsley County High School. He attended Lee County High School in nearby Beattyville, Kentucky, a town of just two square miles and 1,307 people, where the most exciting thing to happen every year is perhaps the Woolly Worm Festival on the third weekend after the first Monday in October. Owsley County High School is Cody's *rival* high school.

"I cannot express the bitter hatred between our two schools," Cody says with the fervor of a high-school athlete who wants to crush his opponent. As a boy growing up in Lee County, he was raised to hate Owsley County.

So why was Cody Johnson, a runner from the fierce, rival-county school, being honored at Owsley County High School's senior day? To understand the reason, we need to understand how competition and cooperation shaped our evolution.

Competition is in our DNA. Many evolutionary biologists believe that the primary pressure driving human sociality is competition from other human groups. Two types of species cannot share the same land. Thus, early humans must have competed against their immediate ancestor for land, just as did modern humans with their immediate ancestor. Scientists argue that, by competing within their own species, humans support the chances for success of their biological information in future generations. Therefore, it is likely that humans competed for their reproductive success primarily with others within their own species. Most followers of Charles Darwin believe that humans do not perform behaviors that are for the good of their species. Darwin's theory of natural selection favors selfish behavior, because altruistic acts only serve to increase the recipient's reproductive success while decreasing that of the donor. Without competition, there is no incentive for organisms to carry a new-and-advantageous gene mutation over older organisms not carrying such a gene. Thus, without competition, there wouldn't be natural selection or an upward trend in evolution. Survival of the fittest.

But it's not that simple. Perusing through books on anthropology and evolution, one comes across the word *cooperation* just as often as *competition*. A number of evolutionary biologists and anthropologists have suggested that cooperation, rather than competition, has been the chief factor in evolution. The word *competition* itself comes from the Latin word *competere*—to seek or achieve together. When we compete, we seek to achieve something together, for the greater good of our species rather than for the individual. Early humans had to cooperate in order to survive. The use of warning cries when enemies approached, submission to the leadership of the strongest male, hunting in packs—all these behaviors exemplified man's need to cooperate. Cooperation and competition happen together. Cody Johnson and Logan Campbell are not the exception to the rule. They *are* the rule. And they are the key to better runs.

During Cody's sophomore cross-country season, he and Logan continued to run neck and neck throughout every race, with the outcome of all of them being decided in the final half-mile. "We developed a strong friendship out of this rivalry," Cody says.

With no one else at their level to run with in their small communities, they started training together. They lived only eleven miles apart.

All this time—from seventh grade through his sophomore year of high school—Cody coached himself. In his junior year, his high-school coach didn't even show up to many of the races. That year, he placed 25th at the Kentucky State Cross Country Championships.

One day, he got an invitation from Sylvia Havicus, the cross-country and track coach at Owsley County High School, to practice with her team during the summer before his senior year.

"I couldn't believe it," Cody says. "I went to practice with them every opportunity that I could." Coach Havicus even let him ride the bus with her team to cross-country races on the weekends that he otherwise wouldn't have been able to run.

"I basically became an unofficial member of my rival school's team," Cody says. Coach Havicus included Cody in local newspaper articles written about the team and honored him at the team's senior day in his senior season, because his own coach had never honored his senior runners before.

"It was truly amazing," Cody says. "This changed me deeply as a person, becoming more passionate about running, as well as making me more humble and hard-working."

In Cody's junior year, he tried to convince the school district to revive his high school's track-and-field program, which had been defunct for eight years. They said no. Cody kept trying. The district gave in. But there was one big problem—no teacher in his school district wanted to coach track and field. The district finally found someone to supervise the kids, and Cody himself acted as the de facto coach while he also competed—a lot to take on for a high-school junior. He recruited enough athletes to the team that they could compete at a few local track meets. He did the same thing his senior year, which would be his best year yet, thanks to a fourth grader.

Slow Runs

I leave my home at 7:00 a.m., my lime green T-shirt highlighted by the early morning sunlight peeking over the mountain. I yawn. I nod good morning to my neighbor, who's out watering her plants, and I begin. Each run is a new beginning. Within the first few minutes, I feel my legs, my breathing, my rhythm. Within those first few minutes, I can tell if the run is going to be good or not. And I strive, every run, to try to do this tremendously simple, yet tremendously complex activity better than I did it yesterday. The first few steps are the most difficult, my tendons and fascia still stiff with the remnants of sleep. After a few minutes, things start to feel loose, and there is no more effort. The steps feel smooth and comfortable, my legs finding the rhythm of their own, internal metronome. The sinoatrial node of my heart dictates a rate of 130 to 135 beats per minute, just enough for me to be aware of its activity. Within minutes, I settle into a pace I can hold forever, and I spend the next hour exploring what that forever is.

Better runs are slow runs. Science tells us that slow runs are good for your health. Humans are aerobic animals, after all. The constant push of oxygen through the blood vessels is a superb stimulus for waking those vessels up and improving perfusion of all your organs.

Science also tells us that slow runs are good for becoming a better runner. Too many runners feel that every day of training needs to be hard, that they have to push the pace and chase a time on a stopwatch. School systems in the US push kids during their developmental years to race too often, and in so doing, they overreach and often become burned out, physically and mentally. If you want to be a faster runner, you first must spend a lot of time running slowly and with control, mastering each run and each level of training before moving on to the next level. Physically, slow runs are relaxing and restorative, building your body up. When done right, and with patience and intention, slow runs lay the foundation for much faster running to come later.

Slow runs also give you the opportunity to enjoy your surroundings and learn about where you are. How many people really know where they are? Running can take you places you can't go with cars. On slow runs, you can explore your environment—you can look at the trees, hear the birds, smell the scents. You can notice things. You can have conversations and laugh with friends.

Once you're fit, running easy is easy. Millions of people all over the world do it every day. Physical benefits aside, running easy and slow, especially when that easy and slow is long enough, has the power to direct your energy and focus inward. Slow runs separate the body from the mind. They give you a chance to think and reflect on things, events, and people in your life. If you're the religious type, you can even have a conversation with God. It can be an emotional and even cathartic experience.

When I run slowly, my mind wanders; it rarely remains on one thought throughout the entire run. Sometimes I think about my problems, or what I want to write about, or the things I have to do that day. Sometimes I think about nothing at all.

Where I run often dictates those thoughts. I've met so many runners who run the same 5-mile loop every day. I even know a few runners who always run on the treadmill, regardless of how nice the weather is. By convenience, I run on neighborhood roads more than anywhere else. The loneliness and solitude of the road lends itself to thought and introspection. Running is a path to self-exploration. I have learned, through my hours on the road, how to become my own psychologist, how to "work in" rather than "work out." The white line of the road is like a best friend. I follow the white line through the local streets. I feel the gentle breeze on my face, evaporating my sweat and cooling me. I smell the fresh fabric softener of someone's laundry as I pass by a house. The best roads are the ones on which there is no one driving, no one walking, no one at all— just the white line and me. It is the white line, like a lover, that I return to every day when things in my life are not going the way I want them to, when things are uncomfortable. And when I finish my run, a never-ending part of my journey, I am content in knowing that the white line will be there again for my run tomorrow.

So many people I meet tell me they ran track or cross-country in high school. Sometimes, it takes a while for that piece of information about them to come to the surface. It seems that something gets lost between the school playground we sprinted around during recess or the track we sprinted around in high school and the cluttered desk at the office. We lose our thrill with speed. Perhaps it's because humans are built more for endurance than we are for speed. Perhaps adults need more time to contemplate while they run, so they need to run slow and easy more often. Perhaps teenagers and young adults don't yet have the life history that begets the need to be contemplative on their runs. All I know is that it's much easier for adults to run slow and easy than it is to run fast and hard. The rapid growth of the half-marathon and marathon can surely attest to that. People find the long, slow pursuit attractive. Humans like to push the limits of endurance, perhaps because when you push the limits of your own endurance, you find out how much you can endure. And that is the greatest metaphor for life. Our ability to endure tough situations, our ability to endure poor health, our ability to endure stress—that is what makes us human.

Fast Runs

If you watch fourth graders run, you'll notice that they run fast for a brief period, stop for an interval to catch their breath, and run fast again for a brief period. They don't instinctively run slowly for long periods of time without stopping. Fourth graders like to run fast. From the time I ran the 50-yard dash as part of the Presidential Physical Fitness Test in fourth grade, I knew I, too, liked to run fast.

Better runs are fast runs. If you want to run faster, run faster. Running slowly all the time, while having numerous physical and psychological benefits, only makes you a slow runner. There is a time and place for fast running. Running fast and hard requires something that running slow and easy doesn't. Both types of running offer great rewards, but unfortunately, many adults shy away from fast running. Kids, on the other hand, love to run fast. Every time I coach a high school or college cross-country or track team, a number of the athletes inevitably ask, "Coach, when are we going to do more speed work?" Kids and young adults love to push themselves. They'd do it every day if they could. It's exciting to watch kids run fast. They crave it. And so do I. I never lost my fascination with speed and what it can do for my body and mind.

Ever since those Presidential Physical Fitness Tests, I've been better at shorter races than longer ones. I like running fast and intensely. It suits my intense personality. Now in my forties, I'm afraid to let go of the speed of my youth. So I often go to the track to run fast. It's fun to run fast. It's a completely different experience than to run slowly. It allows us to let go, to feel powerful and strong, to recruit fast-twitch muscle fibers that are dormant the rest of the day. The funny thing about muscle fibers is that their recruitment is dictated by what we need to perform the task. If we never run fast, we never recruit the fast-twitch fibers, unless we run long enough to fully exhaust our slow-twitch fibers, in which case the fast-twitch fibers are recruited to pick up the slack. When we run fast, however, we recruit nearly everything in our arsenal—slow-twitch *and* fast-twitch fibers. Use it or lose it, as the saying goes.

The other funny thing about muscle fibers is that, if we pay close-enough attention, we can *feel* the difference between recruiting slow-twitch and fast-twitch muscle fibers. The quick steps create a high-energy, aggressive, floating feeling. The scenery in our peripheral vision moves past us quicker. Quick, light steps pop off the ground, like a Kenyan runner on a pogo stick. Pop, pop. There's a smoothness and poetry to the motion that rivals any other athletic movement. When I run fast, I am a caged animal with the door of my cage left open. Fast runs make us free.

Long Runs

Humans have a compelling interest with endurance. We romanticize the stories of Pheidippides and Everest climbers, of Ironman triathletes and ultramarathon runners, envious of their feats. Even non-runners watch marathons and wonder how and why. If there is one thing I know about running and about people who run, it is much easier for people to run long distances, slowly, than it is for them to run short distances, quickly. Every time I go to the track to do an interval workout myself, I'm the only one there. But when I go for easy runs around the neighborhood, I see many people doing the same thing. The explosion in popularity of the marathon and half-marathon races in the US and around the world attests to the same thing: people like running long distances, perhaps because running long distances challenges human endurance. People are more attracted to endurance than speed. There may be many reasons for this. Perhaps people think that if they are not fast to begin with, running fast is not for them. People tend to associate speed with being an athlete, and many (most) people don't see themselves as athletes. Also, people who are overweight and out of shape have difficulty tolerating the physical discomfort that comes with an interval workout. Perhaps people think that anyone can run slowly, so the challenge to run is directed into running slowly for as long as possible—to endure rather than to sprint.

Better runs are long runs, long enough that you learn things you don't know and feel things you don't otherwise feel. I have come to the conclusion that there is not too much in life that a 20-mile run can't fix. On long runs, I work in rather than work out. Long runs change how I perceive what I'm doing. Initially, I see and hear everything. My senses are heightened as I follow the white line of the road through neighborhood streets, a nearby park, or a bike path. I hear a quiet, electric car approaching from behind me. If I run with someone, I listen to my running partner and contribute to the conversation, perhaps even laughing at his dirty jokes. As I begin to fatigue, I go from being aware of my environment and my running partner to being intimately connected to my body. I no longer hear the car approaching or notice the pothole in the street.

I feel the effort of each fatiguing muscle, low on fuel, trying to make yet another contraction. I begin to feel alone and vulnerable, each stride drawing me deeper into myself, further from civilization, closer to discovery. I don't want to talk to anyone.

Through my hours on the road, I become anything or anyone I want. And what I want, more than anything else, is to become a better version of myself. I work through the hard patches, because I believe, deep down, that it is the path to become better and be proud of myself. Not a bad way to spend a Sunday morning.

Paced Runs

I used to coach a talented runner who ran the first mile of every race too fast, only to slow down dramatically during the latter segments and end up disappointed with the result. He thought he was better than his workouts, and he let his competitive spirit and pre-race adrenaline obscure his knowledge of his true fitness level. It was frustrating to watch him start off so well and get slower with each successive lap of the track. It was only after he understood proper pacing and learned how to control himself that he saw the level of success we both knew he could attain.

Better runs are paced runs. I spend a lot of time talking to runners about pace. The single, biggest mistake runners make when they race or do interval workouts is that they start out too fast, way above their fitness level. They either ignore or do not learn from their training a realistically sustainable pace for the entire race. The faster you run the first half of a race, the more your muscles rely on oxygen-independent (anaerobic) metabolism to generate energy. With the greater reliance on oxygen-independent metabolism and muscular work comes an increase in muscle and blood acidosis and the accumulation of metabolites that cause fatigue. So you don't want to run too far above that line so early in the race or workout. Whether the race is a mile or a marathon, you can't put running time in the bank. You will end up losing more time in the end than what you gained by being ahead of schedule in the beginning. No matter how strong your will is to push through the pain, the metabolic condition caused by running too fast, too early will force you to slow down during subsequent stages of the race. Our muscles fatigue for a reason—so we slow down to protect them from damage.

Approach all of your workouts and races with a pace and a mindset that enable you to run a negative split—the second half slightly faster than the first half. To negative split a race requires accurate knowledge of your fitness level, confidence to stick to your plan when other runners start at too fast a pace, and a good dose of self-restraint. The most economical racing strategy, when you want to achieve a specific time rather than a specific place, is to prevent large fluctuations in pace and run as evenly as possible until you near the finish.

To become a better runner, pace is one of the best things you can learn about yourself. One of the runners I coach wrote to me in an email after running a solid, 9-mile tempo run, "I have learned (and continue to learn) about my pacing. If I push myself to a preset pace when my body is not ready, my entire workout (or race) seems to suffer. My body tells me when it is okay to speed up. If I listen, like I did today, I perform better, using less effort for the same pace. If I don't listen, I never seem to gain the fluidity that I am always trying to achieve in training runs and races." Paced runs teach us the art of self-control, of rationing our efforts for the long haul. Become a master of the pace, and you become a master of yourself.

Listen to your inner runner. When you run a race, ask yourself within the first mile (or the first lap or two of a track race), "Can I really hold this pace the entire way?" Be honest with yourself. If the answer is yes, then go for it. If the answer is no, then back off the pace, so you can have a better race. The best workouts and races come when you are in control of them and yourself the whole time and able to run faster in the closing stages, rather than when the workout or race is controlling you and you're just hanging on to the pace, waiting for the finish line.

Becoming a better runner means becoming intimately familiar with different paces and how your body feels. If you can develop an internal clock, it will prevent you from starting races too fast. You'll become more aware of what you're doing in your training runs and races, rather than just throwing caution to the wind and hoping for the best. Proper pacing is vital for success in most races, becoming more important the longer the race. In the marathon, for example, deviating from your average race pace by more than 2 percent is metabolically more costly than deviating by more. In learning what different paces feel like, get to the point that if someone were to say to you, "Run at 5K-race pace," you are able to run at 5K-race pace without looking at your watch. To accomplish this, I sometimes take my runners' watches away from them when they run workouts on the track and give them feedback only from my stopwatch every lap, so they can learn the pace of the workout. Use your workouts to learn a sense of pace. Tracks are invaluable for this. When you do a workout on the track, you can monitor the pace every 100 meters, because tracks are marked in 100-meter segments. If you're not good at pacing, calculate the pace of your workout for every 100 meters, and look at your watch at each marking. Make adjustments to the pace if you're too fast or too slow. After you have done that for a few workouts, look at your watch every 200 meters, then every 300 meters, and then every 400 meters. For longer races like the marathon, do some of your runs on marked paths and practice pace by looking at your watch every mile or every other mile. Over time, you'll acquire a keen sense of pacing that will rival a metronome.

Running includes many internal rhythms, all with their own unique paces that work together. Your heart, your stride, your arm swing, and your breath are all rhythms that are intricately controlled and modified, and define the intensity and feeling of your runs. As you increase your pace from a slow jog to a fast run, heart rate quickens to send more blood to the working muscles to match your muscles' demand for oxygen. Stride rate increases, accompanied by a longer stride to quicken the pace. Arm swing increases by exactly the same amount as the stride rate to balance what the legs are doing and appease Isaac Newton that every action must have an equal and opposite reaction. Breathing rate increases, accompanied by deeper breaths to keep pace with the heart rate and exhale the carbon dioxide that is accumulating in your blood from an increase in metabolic activity. When the run goes right, all of these rhythms—the heart, the stride, the arm swing, the breath—align to create not just a better run, but a better experience.

Breath Runs

When we run, we notice our breath from our very first steps. It is perhaps the most sensitive marker that tells us how hard we're running. There's nothing much better than the feeling of a hard run that makes you breathe more than you ever thought you could. If you've ever done an interval workout at altitude, the sense of breathing that you experience is literally breathtaking. It makes us aware of how closely breathing is connected to our life.

The increased breathing at altitude, even when you're not running, is the obvious indication of a number of subtle changes in your body—including reductions in the oxygen content of your blood, blood plasma, total blood volume, and stroke volume, and increases in fluid loss, resting heart rate, and resting metabolic rate. When I run at altitude, I am more than a runner; I am the personification of physiology.

Better runs are those that are all about your breath. One would think that running is all about breathing. After all, it's through our lungs that we get the oxygen our leg muscles use to run. Many new runners complain that they can't breathe when they start running around the block or on the treadmill and are forced to stop so they can catch their breath. They get frustrated with their lungs, because they perceive them to limit their ability to run. Indeed, getting in enough air and controlling their breath is foremost on their minds. As they run, they huff and puff and nearly blow their Nikes off. The perceived effort is often difficult, because as runners, we link our effort to how hard we're breathing—we know we're working hard when we breathe hard. The challenge of controlling the breath is one of the main reasons people give up on becoming a runner.

It's a marvel of physiology that enough air gets into our bodies, with our nostrils being no larger than the size of a pea. Even the space between semi-pursed lips is small considering the physiological demand for oxygen when we run. A large man who, at rest, breathes about half a liter of air per breath and about six liters of air per minute, breathes nearly 200 liters per minute while running hard. That's 53 gallons of air entering the lungs each minute. Try filling a hose with 53 gallons of water in one minute. Gives you a lot more respect for the lungs and the elegant process of diffusion.

There is an ancient breathing technique associated with yoga called prānāyāma, which means "the control of breath." Among yogis, air is the primary source of prāna, a physiological, psychological, and spiritual force that permeates the universe and is manifested in humans through the phenomenon of breathing. Masters and students of yoga believe that controlling the breath by practicing prānāyāma clears the mind and provides a sense of well-being.

Controlling the breath may have greater implications than the yogis imagined. When you run, you may notice that your breaths often fall in sync with your steps. This interesting characteristic, which was the subject of my doctoral dissertation research, happens without us even thinking about it. Runners, especially those of the four-legged variety, entrain their breathing rhythm to the rhythm of their limb movement. Entrainment, which literally means "drawn along with another," refers to the condition of one variable being forced to keep pace with another.

In animals that run on four legs, the movement of their chest cavity when they breathe actually assists the movement of their forelimbs, forcing every breath to occur with every step. Human entrainment of breathing to stride rate is a bit more variable, given the greater anatomical separation between our chest cavity and our legs. But it happens more often as you become more experienced with running. As ultramarathoner and zoologist Bernd Heinrich, PhD, writes in his book, *Why We Run*,

> The rhythm of my footsteps is steady, unvarying . . . it is unconsciously timed with my breathing. . . . Three steps with one long inspiration, a fourth step and a quick expiration. Over and over and over again. My mantra.

As you become a proficient runner, the stride rhythm, in effect, controls the breath—the runner's version of prāṇāyāma.

Awareness Runs

When I watched Michael Jordan play basketball, I was amazed at how he moved his body over the court, got past defenders, and drove toward the basket. It was as if each of his individual movements were scripted, even though he was really making them up at that instant, his body knowing what to do to be successful. He was able to see openings on the court, just as great running backs are able to see openings on the football field and cut sharply from one direction to another. His body knew and felt its position in space and time. Every movement was automatic. Give him the ball, and his body knew what to do with it. Michael Jordan had a great kinesthetic sense. He was intimately aware of his movements.

On the other side of the movement spectrum is the infant just learning to walk, whose brain must concentrate on taking a single step forward. The infant is beginning to learn his body and how it moves. He is developing a basic kinesthetic sense, slowly becoming aware of his movements.

Kinesthetics describes the sense of detecting the position, weight, or movement of the muscles, tendons, and joints. The word comes from the Greek word, *kinein*, to move. It is the root of the words kinesiology, the study of movement; kinematics, the branch of science that studies the motion of a body with consideration to its position, velocity, and acceleration; and kinetics, the branch of science that studies the forces produced by and acting on a moving body. A child, whose brain is just beginning to write the motor pattern for walking, initially has a poor kinesthetic sense, while elite athletes have a great one. Having a good kinesthetic sense means knowing where your body is in space and time as it moves through those two dimensions with incredible ease and fluidity. It is beautiful to watch.

But it is hard to emulate. Many of us have tried to drive to the basket like Michael Jordan, take a slap shot like Wayne Gretzky, drive a ball off the tee like Tiger Woods, sprint like

Usain Bolt, or run a marathon like Haile Gebrselassie. We compare our actions to those of elite athletes and wonder how they can make their movements look so easy, as we labor in our attempts. And we notice, through the flurry of slam dunks and goals and tee shots and gold medals, that there is one thing they all have in common—the unfaltering skill to move their bodies perfectly to suit the task.

The ultimate reason why sport is so engaging to the spectator is that it is a form—perhaps the highest form—of art. And the athlete is the master artist, the Picasso. But in sport, as distinct from art, everything actually happens—the movements of the athletes are real, happening in the moment, right before our eyes. And, despite the similarities of movements, each action of the athlete is unique and virtually unrepeatable. The manipulation of the human body to perform beautifully complex movements is one of the most aesthetically pleasing sights in this world. At least to me.

We can learn a lot from the athletes we watch. The process of training necessarily makes us more aware of our bodies and how they perform. The greater awareness improves our kinesthetic sense. Maybe that is why I appreciate running so much—for its constant state of awareness. Putting one foot in front of the other is, after all, one of the most basic movements humans make. It is the purest form of sport. It is the essence of kinesthetics.

Better runs are those during which you're aware of your movements and everything going on around you and inside of you. Rather than worry about your pace or become a slave to the technology of running, make your runs better by feeling your runs and improving your own kinesthetic awareness. Feel your foot come into contact with the ground, and see if you can become aware of which part of your foot touches the ground first. Become aware of where your hips are in relation to your legs. Feel your foot land directly underneath your hips. Feel your large quadriceps muscles stabilize your leg on the ground. Feel your foot leave the ground like a spring when you push off. Feel your hamstring muscles contract to flex your leg as your heel comes close to your butt. Feel the air on your face as you effortlessly move over the ground. The more aware you can become of what your body is doing, the greater control you'll have over your movements, and the better runner you'll be.

Also become an expert at what different paces feel like. Get to the point where someone can say, "Go run at 8-minute pace," and you can do it without looking at your watch or GPS. Run faster than you normally do, and see how that feels. To most people, it usually feels harder, especially if they're not used to faster running. Harder running doesn't always translate into faster running. Faster running comes when we don't try as hard, when we are relaxed, when we are so well trained that the effort is almost effortless. Of course, we are still moving our legs and pumping our arms and breathing deeply, but there is a fluidity of movement, a feeling we achieve when we don't muscle our way through the workout or race. The pace comes to us, rather than us forcing our way to it.

Runners, perhaps more than any other type of athlete, or even any other type of person, are intimately aware of how they feel. And how a runner physically feels affects him or her psychologically. "How do you feel?" is, by far, the question I ask most often of the runners I coach. I can tell by a verbal or nonverbal response how good the workout or race will be. How a runner feels during any given run or workout, in the moments before or during any given race, or at any given moment in his or her life, is a big part of not only how he or she performs, but of his or her outlook on life. Runners, truth be told, are very sensitive people. We feel things deeply. We are toughened by the effort we put forth, by the emotional investment we make, and we care about the outcome. We put our hearts into what we do. I can't speak for all runners, but for this runner, how my legs feel when they move over the earth is the single, most influential variable in my life. When my legs feel light and peppy and fast, I feel great inside, like my effort and investment are paying off, and I take a positive approach to everything else in my life. When my legs feel heavy and flat and slow, I don't feel so good inside; I question what the heck I am doing wrong, and everything else in my life seems to be more difficult.

When we become kinesthetically aware of our movements and pace, we run better races, because we're able to self-govern our running efforts, including the common mistake nearly all runners make of running too fast in the early stages of races. More importantly, however, developing an inner GPS and becoming an expert "feeler" of our runs gives us a whole new experience. We are no longer a pace or a heart rate or a stride rate. The data and the feeling become one and the same. We are the run.

Emotional Runs

If you stand near the finish line of a major marathon, you'll notice something very peculiar. Grown men and women who are the essence of vitality and the strength of human will cry as they cross the finish line. Why do they do this?

Better runs are emotional runs. The runs that stir something inside of us. The runs that make us aware that we are much more than flesh and biochemistry. When we run, we are raw, vulnerable, outside in the elements with nothing to protect us except our own will and courage.

I once coached a high-school runner who got so emotional during interval workouts that she would nearly cry during them. She could hardly jog in between each rep, because it's hard to jog when you're crying. I would ask her what's wrong, and she would say, "I don't know." After the workout, she said she was overwhelmed by how many reps she still had to run. She would get through eight reps and think, "I still have eight more to go." She let her head get ahead of her, and the difficulty and volume of the workout caused her to become emotional about it. So we tried a few tricks. I asked her to think about one rep at a time and not worry about how many were left to run. I asked her to count her steps when she ran each lap of the track and not think about anything else. I asked her to focus on her arm swing, aggressively swinging her arms back and forth. I asked her to imagine her fiercest competitor running right in front of her and focus on running with her. I asked her to stop thinking about anything at all and just run.

One of the many values of hard workouts is the opportunity to practice emotional control and find the courage to complete them. There will always be a voice inside of us that says, "This is hard," or "This hurts," or "I want to stop." We can either let that voice get the best of us, or we can work on mastering ourselves and our emotions. As runners, we need to harness the power of our emotions and use them to help us work through the discomfort of the moment and become who we want to be. Through experience and training, we learn how to do that.

Hard, physical effort taps into something visceral in us. It's animalistic. It's powerful. We feel it in a way we don't feel other things. It's often easy to get caught up in the moment. When we run with emotion, it can bring us to places we never thought possible. Sometimes when I race, I draw on the deep emotions I have about losing my parents. In those moments, I am in a place where no one knows, where no one can be but me. It is a place made up of anger, fear, emotional distress, love. It is a cathartic experience. I draw on those emotions to fulfill my physical potential. Like the person who lets go and yells in the middle of the forest or in the presence of a passing train, I yell through my physical effort. It is so draining that I can do it only on certain occasions. But on those occasions that I do, they are among my best as a runner.

Olympic runner Glenn Cunningham, who held the world mile record in the 1930s, once said, "[The runner's] adversary lies within him, in his ability, with brain and heart, to master himself and his emotions." Mastering your emotions is absolutely essential to being the best runner you can be. Next time you run a race, draw on deeper emotions to discover what you can achieve.

Cross-Country and Trail Runs

From my very first cross-country race as a freshman in high school, I knew it was something special. The crispness of the autumn air, the morning dew on the grass, the colored leaves at the start of the season, and the leaves on the ground by the season's end, uphills, downhills, the starting line of 200 runners anxiously awaiting the starter's gun, the crackling of the 200 pairs of spikes on the patches of pavement between fields of grass and dirt trails, and one winner at the end of the race; there's nothing quite like it.

Better runs are cross-country and trail runs. When I run in the woods or on back-country trails, I feel like I'm escaping society, and kick myself for not doing it more often. The dirt-and-pebbled path becomes my line of discovery. All of my senses are heightened. The autumn leaves blend to form a kaleidoscope of magnificent colors; shades of orange, brown, red, green, yellow, and purple follow me on my route. The breeze rustles the leaves of the dense trees, sounding like the fall of a light rain. Each stride draws me deeper into the woods. I can lose myself on the trails, always trusting that, by the end of the run, I will find exactly where I am. I can choose whichever path I want. The trails remind me that I can choose whichever path I want in my life as well. We're not obligated to stay on the path we're on.

Pure happiness, Sigmund Freud suggested, is when you take your foot out from beneath the covers in the middle of winter and then place it back in. When you run off-road, on trails and mountains and cross-country, pure happiness is when you take your foot out from beneath the covers and leave it out, risking what's uncomfortable. In this setting, pure happiness is not found in satisfying comfort; it is found in dealing with discomfort. You are out in nature, exposed and vulnerable to the elements. I feel like I own the land I'm running on. Running free in the middle of nowhere is some of the best running I've ever done. With no one in sight, I am at peace.

Cross-country and trail running is a great way to become part of the earth's natural backdrop, to run as you feel, and do some quality speed work without the confines and monotony of the track. One of my favorite cross-country workouts is one that I learned from my college coach—the Tee to Green Fartlek. On a golf course, starting at the first tee, run hard from the tee to the green, and recover by jogging from the green to the next tee. Run as many holes of the golf course as is reasonable for your ability and fitness level. Given the short distance between a golf course green and the next tee, compared to between a tee and the green, the recovery periods are short in this workout compared to the faster efforts, so you have to be careful about pushing the pace early in the workout and run very easy during the short recovery periods. It's a great, fun workout in a beautiful setting.

Track Runs

It's Tuesday evening. Time for my interval workout. I jog over to the track at the local high school, the butterflies in my stomach fluttering faster now, their activity an obvious reminder now of what had been simmering all day. I warm up for a couple of miles, do some dynamic stretching and a few 100-meter strides, all the while aware of how my legs feel, trying to determine whether what's to come will be a good experience or a difficult one.

I start the first rep around the track, and my heart pounds within my chest, as cardiac output—a product of heart rate and stroke volume—rises rapidly to meet the muscles' demand for oxygen. The rate and depth of my breathing also rise rapidly to exhale the carbon dioxide accumulating in my blood from the greater metabolic activity and, to a lesser extent that becomes more prominent when running at altitude, to inhale more oxygen with each breath.

As I continue to run around the track, my whole life becomes focused in my lane. Everything I do and everything I am is condensed between the two white lane lines that contain my effort around the 400-meter track. It is the most personal experience I will have all day. For the next thirty minutes, this four-foot width becomes a microcosm of my life. Nothing else matters except what occurs between the two lines. I am acutely aware of every muscle contraction, every heartbeat, every breath. My muscles and blood become acidic because of the hydrogen ions accumulating from the chemical reactions that provide the energy for muscle contraction. The faster and stronger the muscle contractions, the more hydrogen ions and other metabolites, like potassium and phosphate, accumulate, and the more my muscles fatigue. I turn my mind inward, focusing on the effort, focusing on my stride, attacking the rubberized track surface with each step, and swinging my arms from their strong deltoid pendulum. I run an exact distance in an exact time. Time matters on the track. Effort matters.

After running 400 meters, I slow my pace to a jog to recover for a couple of minutes, and my very rapid breathing rate and heart rate begin to decline. Blood quickly returns to my heart—filling the left ventricle that is rapidly slowing its rate of beating—and is ejected back out again with a forceful pump, spiking my heart's stroke volume. After two minutes of jogging, and with my heart rate still elevated, I run fast for another lap, at the pace I could hold for just one mile in a race. Each rep is another mini-challenge to face between those two lane lines. But I don't think about what's to come. All that matters is the lap I'm running now. Like blinders on a skittish horse, I focus on my lane, pushing the rubber under my feet behind me with the powerful ball of my foot, reaching for the next step. My legs come off the final turn of the track like a slingshot into the homestretch. I pump my arms and lift my heavy, acidic legs off the track—*pick them up, put them down*—all the while trying to maintain composure and stay as relaxed as possible, reminding myself of all the cues I give to those I coach. The thoughts and cues run through my head as quickly as my legs move across the track. With each rep, the workout becomes physically and mentally more difficult to tolerate, like a needle that touches the skin and penetrates deeper and deeper. Each rep completed in the designated time is a major victory. It's an uncomfortable experience, to be sure—my cardiovascular and muscular systems pushed to their limits—but one that teaches me about myself. After I complete the last rep and jog off the track to begin my cool-down, I look back at the track, as if to look at the work I'd just completed.

Better runs are track runs. There's something powerful and fast about running on a track. The way my shoes grip the track's rubber surface, the power and smooth coordination of my muscles, the crispness of my stride, the exactness of the distance, the way my feet feel as they push against the track's surface, all come together to enhance my running experience. Like a child at play. If running in the woods or on the road is about running within myself, then running on the track is about running outside of myself. It is where I ask myself to bring the effort out. The internally reserved experience of a slow, easy run on the open road or the trails becomes an outwardly aggressive experience on the enclosed track.

Despite all of the attention on high-intensity interval training for its time-saving effectiveness in improving fitness, it's much easier for people to go long and slow than to go short and fast. Every time I go to the track to run, there are no other runners around. It's a shame, because there is so much fitness to be gained and so much to learn about oneself on the track.

When people relocate to a different place, some people want to be near the beach, or a hospital, or a church, or a park for their kids. Call me silly, but every time I have moved, I have always made sure I live close to a track.

The track tells me the truth about myself, whether or not I want to hear it. It tells me my current fitness, because I can't hide from the stopwatch—I'm given the exact time for an exact distance. It tells me whether, on that day, I'm willing to push the pace. The track challenges me to answer myself. It is where I find out who I really am. Every runner should experience what it's like to run fast on a track.

Treadmill Runs

I once coached a runner who, in her late twenties, started her life as a runner on the treadmill. She told me that when she first started running, she was intimidated about running outside. There's a certain comfort about the controlled environment of the treadmill. It's safe. If anything happens, you're not miles from home. You can't get lost on a treadmill, other than in your thoughts.

Better runs are treadmill runs. Treadmills have been around for a long time. The original ones, called treadwheels, were animal-powered motors used for farming. The modern version of the treadmill, historically used to punish misbehaving prison inmates, was first used for exercise in 1952, when doctors Robert Bruce and Wayne Quinton at the University of Washington in Seattle had their patients walk on it, so they could monitor the patients' heart function. The treadmill has since become the most popular piece of cardio equipment. And for good reason—when it comes to burning calories and losing weight, research has shown that the treadmill is the top piece of cardio equipment. However, treadmill running incurs a lower metabolic energy cost (*i.e.*, you use less energy and burn fewer calories) compared to running over ground, particularly at faster speeds. When you run on a treadmill, there is no air resistance, and your muscles don't have to work as hard, because the treadmill belt pulls your leg back as it lands. For this reason, some runners think the treadmill feels easier than running outdoors.

I get asked all the time about running on treadmills. Although I've always been in favor of running outside over a treadmill, I believe people should run wherever is going to give them the best workout that day. So, if running outside is going to hurt your workout because of the weather, then run on a treadmill.

During cold, snowy months, treadmills offer a great option to maintain your running routine and improve your fitness. Given the ability to manipulate the speed and grade, treadmills offer many great workout options. The controlled environment can make your workouts even better, because you can focus all of your attention on the effort.

One of the best uses of the treadmill is to run hills. On a treadmill, you can manually manipulate the grades of the hills, the speeds you run up and down them, and how many hills you run. You can also manipulate uphill and downhill running on treadmills for a challenging workout that can specifically prepare you for races that have both uphills and downhills.

For hill rep workouts, treadmills offer the advantage of not having to run back down the hill, which can cause a lot of muscle soreness and slow your recovery from the workout. Running on a treadmill allows you to focus just on the uphill portion.

I admit, if I'm not doing a specific workout, like hill reps or intervals, I find treadmill running boring. I need something to distract me. It seems many people feel the same way, given how every fitness center has television screens either on their walls, hanging from the ceiling, or even built into the treadmills themselves for people to watch while they run. I know some runners who create a movie theater in their basement with their treadmill the only "seat" in the theater. I suppose if I owned a treadmill, I would do that, too.

Beyond the precise workouts that you can get on treadmills, they also offer a chance to think. There's something about the monotony of running on a treadmill—the repetitive motion, the constant speed, the sound of the belt as your feet land, the hum of the motor—that puts you in a trance. It's just you and the rhythm of the run—your breath, your legs, your feet, your heartbeat.

Morning Runs

In late spring of 2000, I attended the California High School State Track and Field Championships at Cerritos College with a few athletes who qualified from the high-school team I was coaching in San Francisco. One morning, before heading over to the track with the athletes, I left the hotel to go for a run. Having never been to Cerritos before, I didn't know where to run, so I did what I always do when I run in a foreign place—I chose a direction and went exploring. Cerritos, at least in the area of my hotel, was busy with traffic, so I started out running on the sidewalk along the street until I could find a quieter place to run. After a little while, I came upon a collection of buildings surrounded by a gate that resembled a campus, so I entered the open gate, thinking that it would be a more peaceful place to run than along the sidewalk of the busy street. The campus was pretty quiet. A few people were walking around, accompanied by people with long white coats. As I kept running, I got a strange feeling that this wasn't a college campus. A few minutes later, I realized that I was running on the campus of a psychiatric hospital. "I better get out of here," I thought, lest anyone think I was one of the patients. I quickly turned around to run back the way I came.

As I approached the gated entrance, I heard a voice call out at me. "Excuse me, where are you going?" It was the guard at the gate. What started as amusement with the white coats quickly turned to panic. Was I going to be kept hostage at a mental hospital? Do I have issues after all? Has that voice in my head been real all these years? Sometimes, I admit, I look a little crazy in my running shorts. My shorts! That's it! I felt around my shorts for the hotel-room key card in the pocket, my hands shaking with the excitement of a kid opening his presents on Christmas morning.

"Here," I said to the guard, as I dug into my shorts. "This is my hotel key of where I'm staying. You can call the hotel and ask them."

Luckily, the guard must have thought anyone running in skimpy shorts early in the morning on the campus of a psychiatric hospital must be too crazy even for that place. After giving me a concerned look, he let me go. It certainly made for a funny story later, when I told the high-school kids what had happened to their coach that morning.

Better runs are morning runs. People often assume I run first thing in the morning, as if all runners must be morning runners. Truth is, even though I like the idea of early-morning runs, when the world is brand new, watching the sunrise and enjoying the quiet calm, I've never been a morning runner. Despite my twin brother and me being conceived first thing in the morning, I've never even been a morning person, much less a morning runner. I've been lucky to avoid a job most of my life that has required me to get up early every morning and go to an office. I missed many 8:00 a.m. classes in college, because I couldn't get out of bed. Perhaps that explains why I got a D in physics.

I always have felt better running in the afternoon, especially when it's an intense workout. Unfortunately, almost all races are early in the morning. I have to get to a race extra early, because it takes me some time to wake up my body during my warm-up to get ready to race.

Studies show I'm not alone. Lots of people get Ds in physics. And lots of people perform better later in the day. Research has shown that athletic performance, especially of the high-intensity, anaerobic variety, typically peaks in late afternoon or early evening, in concert with the daily peak in core body temperature later in the day. And the time you wake up makes a difference in your performance, too. There are consistent peak-performance times for early and late risers, which hinge on how many hours you've been awake. Likely due to the influence of hormones, like cortisol, and how they are modulated by our circadian rhythms, early risers—those who wake up around 7:00 a.m.—tend to perform better earlier in the afternoon, while late risers—those who wake up after 9:30 a.m.—perform better later in the evening.

I'm envious of morning runners. I feel like they're getting away with something, that they're able to do something that doesn't come naturally to me. Times that I have run early in the morning have been great experiences. There's a calmness to the early morning that I can't seem to replicate later in the day. The cool, crisp air, the gentle sunlight peeking through the trees, the shadows, the lack of cars on the road, the knowledge that most people are still cuddled up with their blankets, all come together to provide a unique mind-body experience. There's also a strong feeling of accomplishment that accompanies completing a run first thing in the morning. I've always wanted to be one of those people who say, "I get more done before 8:00 a.m. than most people get done in a day." But my circadian rhythm seems to favor the evening. When I was in college, I got into the habit of going to bed late and waking up late, consequently missing those darn 8:00 a.m. physics classes, and the habit has persisted all these years since.

Social Runs

Through the summer of 2013, each Thursday morning I met my friend Pedro for an 8- to 9-mile tempo run at a 6:45 to 6:50 pace around the perimeter of a golf course in Chula Vista, California. Long tempo runs have always been difficult for me. Pedro, a sub three-hour marathoner, is very good at them. Before we started each tempo run, we stood on the side of the road, and Pedro said a prayer for both of us. Over the next hour, he talked about his kids, told me stories, provided motivation, and helped me hold the pace. And he taught me a little about life.

Better runs are social runs. Despite my oftentimes intro-verted, antisocial behavior, every time I run with someone, I'm happy I did so. By running with others, I realize that people can be a source of inspiration, of ideas, of laughter, of stories. After an early Sunday morning run with friends, you can go out for pancakes and talk about your upcoming race or your nagging tendonitis you can't get rid of. Runners like to talk about their runs and races and injuries to other runners. Misery and happiness both love company. Humans are social animals.

There's little doubt that running with others can help you become a better runner. It's the reason why so many elite runners train in groups with other elite runners. It's easier to push yourself when someone is running right next to you, even if neither of you say a word. Group runs offer camaraderie and accountability, resources and a network for information about running, and encouragement and motivation. You'll also feel a sense of belonging to a team if you join a formal group that competes together in races.

When I go from running by myself to running with a group, I become a member of a tribe. Like any other tribe, there are rituals. The pre-run stretches, the congratulations for Mary on her 10K PR last weekend, the announcements about where the pancake breakfast will be. Then we're off on our run. Within a few minutes, little cliques form—the three speedy runners at the front, the girlfriends who want to gab with each other, the guy who wants to talk to the cute girl with the ponytail. Each runner has his or her own reason for being there.

Running with others convinces me that running is not all about me. Perhaps, most of all, social runs give us a chance to share—to share our highs, to share our lows, to share our funny stories, to share our running spirits, to share our passions, and to share our experiences of being runners. Gaining strength from that of others, witnessing their passion, can help bring out the best in us.

Solo Runs

I've never been much of a people person. I'm an introvert by nature, perhaps who Alan Sillitoe had in mind when he wrote about the loneliness of the long-distance runner. Almost all the time, I run alone. Running is my thing, and I don't want anyone to mess with it. It's a rare day that I let someone into my running life. Many runners are finicky about who can share their running time. Why would I want to run with others when I can be by myself to think and create? With everything that is involved with meeting a running group, why would I want to take two hours out of my day to run five miles? I'd rather run alone, thank you.

Better runs are solo runs. Humans are and will always be drawn to the solo run, because life is, ultimately, lived alone, in the light and dark spaces inside of us, no matter how many people we are surrounded by. No matter how close we get to someone—a parent, a child, a spouse—we can never know them fully. We can never know another person the way we know ourselves. We can never be as comfortable—or as uncomfortable—with another person as we are with ourselves.

When I run alone, the world is mine. I don't feel obligated to hold a conversation with someone else. I am not bothered by anyone. I can run anywhere I want, however fast or slowly I want. On solo runs, I can ask myself questions and search inside of myself for answers. I am doing something for myself, without any intrusion from anyone else. The work I'm doing is mine. I own it. I suffer through the intervals on the track. I find peace on the slow, easy runs on the beach or in the woods. By myself. I am empowered by the knowledge that I'm doing something no one else is doing in that same place at that same time. And that time alone makes me a better, more confident person when I'm out in public, interacting with others. One hour, I am completely alone running in the middle of nowhere, and the next hour, I am surrounded by many people in society. I am captivated by that contrast.

No matter how much you like being around other people, we all need that time to be alone, to learn about ourselves, to push ourselves without help from anyone else. On solo runs, we become independent, we become competent, and we have the chance to prove to ourselves that we can do things on our own. We can go to a place deep inside that no one else is privy to and make peace with our emotions. We can let our demons out. When we get right down to it, the most important things in life, the ones during which we discover who we really are, are done alone.

Coached Runs

Running appears to be a simple sport, and as such, we often think we know it all. Running is one of the only sports in which most people who participate don't have a coach. This is even true at the elite level.

A good coach teaches you why to train a certain way, designs a seamless, progressive, systematic program for you, monitors what you're doing, and relieves you of the responsibility of planning your own training, so you can focus on the training itself. A coach can be the greatest asset a runner can have.

Better runs are coached runs. Research shows that people who train under the supervision of a coach see better results than those who don't. Anyone can give you a bunch of workouts. But it takes an expert to design your workouts to cause specific physiological changes and organize them into a progressive, systematic training program that allows you to achieve your potential. Knowing the how and why of your training will go a long way to you becoming a more accomplished runner, because it helps you develop an understanding of the process.

When you try to coach yourself, it's hard to see things the way they really are, because you're too close to the situation. Having an outside pair of eyes is important. A coach can see the whole picture and tell you when to push and when to back off and recover.

Don't underestimate the value of a good coach. A coach can be a trainer, motivator, teacher, source of inspiration, and even a confidant. He or she can guide you to achieve a level of success that cannot be obtained on your own.

A coach can also prepare you to race. He or she can advise you on how to run your races, discuss race strategy with you, and motivate and inspire you to do things that you never thought possible. A coach teach you how to race effectively and help you develop a race strategy, so you can achieve the best result.

Race Runs

It's the last lap of my mile race. I'm hurting, but I can't think about that now. I say to myself, "Go, go, go!" My heart is pounding like a rabid pit bull in my chest. My acidic legs feel like they are no longer attached to the rest of my body. "Go, go, go!" I aggressively attack the Mondo track with my spikes down the backstretch, but I can tell my stride length has drastically shortened from the fatigue. As I come off the last turn into the homestretch for the final 100 meters, I turn as inward as inward goes, and move my arms and legs as fast as

I possibly can. I'm a gazelle running away from a lion attack. "Go, go, go!"

I am on the edge of life and death.

Better runs are races. Races are a chance to put all of the work of training into something of consequence. It is a test of our fitness, a test of our resolve. When you pin that race number to your shirt, you make a promise to yourself and the other runners around you to give your best effort. And when you cross that finish line, you'll know whether or not you kept that promise.

The moments before a race are some of the most anxious moments of my life. They are filled with a kaleidoscope of feelings—nervousness, hope, doubt, excitement, fear, and confidence all at once. Those moments make me feel alive.

When I was a junior in high school, I ran a 5K cross-country race in which I was leading, with a pack of runners from another school right off my shoulder. I was feeling very confident, like I was dictating the pace. With about half a mile to go, once we turned onto a different section of the course, the entire pack of runners went by me as if I were standing still. By the time I realized what had happened, it was too late for me to respond to their move. They were too far ahead for me to catch them before the finish line.

After the race, the coach of the other team came over to me and told me that was their plan all along—they knew I was the best runner on the other team, and they had singled me out before the race as they watched me warm up. They had planned for me to set the pace and do the work for most of the race, and then make their move at a predetermined point, going by me all at once. And I fell for it. I was disappointed that

I didn't win the race after leading it for so long, but I was even more disappointed that I let myself be duped. Their strategy worked, because I didn't see it coming. If there's one race in my career that I wish I could run over again, that race is it, even though it was just a small race against one other school with no championship or big trophy on the line.

There are all kinds of subtle things that go on in a race, just like there are all kinds of subtle things that go on in life, and it takes practice and experience to notice those things. When you run, it's important to stay as relaxed as possible. When we get nervous or stressed or feel pressure, our attention narrows, causing us to concentrate on just a few things at a time. A narrow focus, while important for success, can also cause us to miss important details in our environment if we're not careful. That happened to me in that high-school race, and I'm still kicking myself for it all these years later.

When you race, your body releases hormones that make you hyper-alert, focused, and energized, and a chemical cascade ensues that causes heart rate, breathing rate, and perspiration to increase. Racing gives you the power to observe your surroundings and make detailed assessments about your environment. When you race, be aware of what's going on around you, rather than letting the race pass you by. Be aware of the other runners, how they may be working together, and be ready to react to their moves.

What is it about a race that makes such a disparate group of people come together to do something so similar? Running has the power to bring very different people together for a common cause. Where else can you go to find thousands of people competing in the same event? Running is open to the public—it is the only sport that is accessible on a competitive level to everyone. And it is the only sport in which the general public can compete in the same event at the same time as the best in the world.

When I first started running track and cross-country in school, and for many years after, I defined myself by how fast I ran my races. If I didn't run as fast as I wanted, I would get down on myself. I would mope around for days after a disappointing race. My identity was tied to my race results. Although I still get disappointed when I don't run as fast as I want or think I should, I've slowly and reluctantly realized that I'm not defined by my races. I'm still a great person if I don't run a 4:29 mile or a 2:59 marathon. And so are you.

One of the first questions people will ask you when you tell them you ran a race is, "What time did you run?" The answer is usually, "Not as fast as I wanted." This is especially true of the marathon. When it comes to the marathon, whether they want to qualify for Boston or break five hours, most runners go into the race thinking about a certain time they want to run. And most run slower than they want to.

Putting all your eggs in the time-means-everything basket is a great way to be disappointed if it doesn't work out. Although it's hard to run a race without some expectations, you're much better off if you focus on your performance rather than the outcome. The time on the clock is an outcome. If you focus on your performance, you have a much better chance of achieving the outcome you hoped for.

Except for the few people who have the ability to win races, racing is not about winning. Sure, it feels good to win. I've been fortunate enough to win a number of races in my life, all of which were when I was younger and none of which were of any real consequence, other than how good it made me feel. I fell far short of the Olympic dreams of my youth. No matter what level of runner you are, running is about how much we can put ourselves on the line, literally and figuratively, to measure up against our true selves and shorten the distance between who we are and who we want to be. When we put ourselves on the line and pledge to run as fast as we can, we become vulnerable. We expose ourselves to the one person we matter most to—ourself.

Racing is the best example of living through our bodies. When we race, we push our bodies to their limits. Or at least we hope to. We are given the rare opportunity to act like an animal in the wild, running free and showing our inner strength. Racing, if we do it with our whole heart, forces us to face what is happening right at that moment, in a way that few other experiences do. We give it our all, and we get even more back.

I always tell the runners I coach when going into a race, whether it's a half mile or a marathon, that the most important thing is that they finish the race feeling like they couldn't have done any better on that day. Regardless of the outcome—the time on the clock and the place you finish—what matters most is that you walk away from the race being able to say to others and to yourself that you gave it everything you had. That alone is something to be immensely proud of. That alone is worth the race entry fee.

"Better runs" means a lot of things. It means better movements, better thoughts, better insights, better experiences. It means educating yourself on what makes for good training, so you can train smarter. It means training with a coach or mentor who can guide you and bring out your potential. It means running along the whole continuum of paces, from very slow to very fast. It means running in different places and on different terrain, where you can see different things and give your legs and your mind a variety of stimuli. It means controlling your breathing and syncing it with all of the other rhythms of your body. It means being aware of your surroundings. It means rising to the occasion. It means making a friend out of a rival and pursuing something together for a greater good. It means enjoying the experience that each run gives you. To be better runners, we must start by running better.

Running is very connective. It connects us to nature. Whenever we want, we can play hooky from life and go explore our environment. We run on the beach, up a mountain, or in a park; we run around a lake, in the woods, or around our neighborhood. We run in the wild and share the land with other animals.

Running connects us to people. When I'm in a crowded coffee shop or restaurant, where all the surrounding conversations blend together, I always hear when someone talks about running. The word "run" stands out for me. My ear always catches the word on someone's tongue, and I start talking to people I never would have talked to otherwise. We run with friends who share their stories, who confide in us, who tell us jokes, who introduce us to other people to do business with, make friends with, or even to marry. No matter how different people are from one another, the common interest of running connects us. Through running, we understand each other and come to know what it means to compete. In other runners, we see ourselves.

Running connects us to our bodies. The human experience is physical. Every single thing we do, every single day is attached to our physical being. To live life fully, we must fully live on a physical level. Every step we run, we are aware of the physicality of our motions, from the strong contractions of our quads to the rubbing of our pinky toe against the tiny hole in our sock. Things that we are not aware of the rest of the day, we become hyper-aware of when we run. That's why I deeply believe that running *is* for everyone. Because it is the best expression of our physicality. Research shows that people experience sport activities substantially more positively than the rest of everyday life. Perhaps that's because, through running, we fulfill our destiny as physical beings, and on the foundation of a fitter physical being, we can build a better life.

Running connects us to our effort. There is a direct relationship between how hard we try and how fast our feet move across the ground. We push the pace, and we feel the effort we're making. We can choose to challenge ourselves on any given day, at any given moment during our runs. We can polarize and play with our training by making our slow runs slower, our fast runs faster, our long runs longer. Running enables us to push ourselves past limits we thought we had.

Running connects us to our souls. When we run, we feel like we are living the life we are supposed to live and carrying out what Aristotle called the "actus primus," the first actuality, of our bodies. Running takes us beyond Aristotle and transcends our flesh and our physical efforts, connecting us to the immortal part of ourselves that science and its neuroimaging techniques have been unable to touch.

There are so many different types of runs, so many places we can do them, and so many things we can experience from them. Running is the purest of all sports—there is no equipment, no special clothing, and nothing to encumber you. It's just you and the open road. And you can run wherever you want. What other physical activity can you do wherever you go in the world? I have run past cows on rural roads in State College, Pennsylvania, around the Opera House in Sydney, along the hot, humid beaches in Tel Aviv, with icicles formed on my face mask from my breath in Calgary, through pollution and the smell of spices in Bangkok and Jakarta, gasping for breath on the Sandia Mountains in Albuquerque, and darting through traffic in Times Square in New York. I even once stashed my luggage in an airport locker and ran around Orlando Airport during a layover, coming as close as one could be to the runways without being part of the flight crew. Running is the best way to explore the world. I find running all over the world to be fluid with life and the constant journey that feeds our souls with desire and passion. With all these different, entertaining experiences, who needs the Kardashians?

Each type and each place we run offers different insights from which to discover new lines of thinking, to discover ourselves. Each of these types of runs is a better run for its own rewards. We become our runs. We become the landscape of our runs. We become the thoughts and insights and experiences we have on our runs. Run to find new adventure and be changed by the experiences and sights you encounter.

An important component of the value of physical activity is the experience it provides. Even if it means getting caught on the campus of a psychiatric hospital with your only identification being a hotel-room key card in your skimpy-running-shorts pocket.

Under Cody Johnson's leadership, the track-and-field program at Lee County High School grew.

"Coaching these kids to do something I love inspired me to become a better person, more persistent than ever, and led me to become a strong leader," he says. "Coaching as a nineteen-year-old is not easy at all. Running has taught me to be patient." But the work of school, training, competing, reviving a track-and-field team where there hadn't been one for eight years, and coaching his peers was taking its toll. Cody started to get burned out from it all.

One day during his senior cross-country season, he spotted a kid running named Jacob McCoy. "He really impressed me. He was only in the fourth grade, but I saw that he had potential," Cody says. Cody knew Jacob's father rather well, so he asked if Jacob wanted to train with him. "He never quit and was always excited to run," Cody says of Jacob. "He was remarkably intelligent and mature for his age. But everyone still called him Baby Jake."

Cody and Baby Jake ran a lot together during that cross-country season, a high-school senior and a fourth grader running side-by-side. In the spring, Cody invited his new protégé to practice with the Lee County High School track-and-field team. Almost immediately, fourth grader Baby Jake outran the distance runners on the team, running the second fastest 1,600-meter time on the team behind Cody.

"Seeing Baby Jake's success inspired me to work hard my senior year when I was burned out on the sport," Cody says. "He was probably the biggest reason for my success that year in cross-country and track. If it weren't for him, I probably wouldn't have won the regional 800-meter race or had much success at all."

On Saturday, November 2, 2013, at Kentucky's Region 7 Cross-Country Championships—the qualifier for the state championships—senior Cody Johnson placed second. His friend Logan Campbell placed first. "It was beyond special, as we had trained together for so long, running local races and going on training runs together on Sundays," Cody says, the excitement of the moment relived in his voice. "My freshman year, we made it our goal to finish first and second in the region."

A week later, on November 9, Cody lined up along 216 other runners, including Logan, on the starting line at the Kentucky State Cross Country Championships. He placed twenty-eighth.

"I have learned that running is a lot like the real world in that you get rewarded by what you put into it," he says. "It requires all of your effort, persistence, and mind. I have also learned that I will never give up on anything. Multiple times I have had my back against the wall with a lack of support from the school system, putting me in a position to coach myself, but I always battled through to succeed, which makes it so much more fulfilling."

Of all the running success Cody had in high school, none of it, he says, made him who he is now. "All of the experiences did. They changed me from being an arrogant, successful runner to being very humble and responsible."

Now a sophomore at Eastern Kentucky University, Cody has changed his major from athletic training to biology education, with a minor in coaching, so moved he has been by his experiences and the people in his life. He says he wants to become a high-school coach. "Running has, without a doubt, become my life thanks to Logan, Coach Havicus, and the experiences I've had. I could go on for days about each of them. Baby Jake is the biggest inspiration for me pursuing a coaching career. Watching his success while training with me was breathtaking and exciting. He made me love coaching. The kid has been my biggest inspiration and doesn't even know it."

When asked what this whole experience has meant to him, Cody speaks with the wisdom of someone twice his age. "I realized that the best things in life can come from unexpected places. Before I met Logan and Coach Havicus, I wouldn't have ever thought about being friends with anybody from rival Owsley County. Now, Coach Havicus, Logan, and his entire family are like my family. Logan and I are like brothers. And I consider myself a member of the Owsley community. I also learned, thanks to Baby Jake, that teaching kids new things that are most precious to you is the best thing in the world. That's why I am now inspired to coach cross-country and track for as long as I can, so that others may have as wonderful an experience as I have had."

Throughout Cody's freshman year of college, which was Logan Campbell's senior year of high school, Cody and Logan continued to train together. In the fall of 2014, it was Logan's turn to be honored at Owsley County High School's senior day. Cody was at the race.

"Running has meant everything to me. It makes me feel so free. It is a way for me to bond with others—those I train with, compete against, and coach in the future."

CREATIVE AND IMAGINATIVE RUNS

"I'M FEELING GOOD NOW, AND I'M GOING TO STICK WITH THAT."

If you run down Haight Street in San Francisco, you'll come across The Gallery, a small art studio with a 1960s-looking storefront, nestled among other 1960s-looking shops in the well-known hippie district of Haight-Ashbury. Inside The Gallery, a fifty-five-year-old, African American man with a gray goatee and a beanie sits on a stool and paints on a canvas. His artwork, much of which depicts scenes of San Francisco, adorns the walls.

Ronnie Goodman is a self-taught artist in San Francisco. He's been painting on and off since he was eight years old. His art, he says, is inspired by the beauty and diversity of San Francisco, balanced with the struggles of human despair.

"With my brush, I try to capture these raw emotions in painted images of the city," he says. "I have a story to tell. I think I have a lot to say. Being an artist is very hard to make a living. The most important thing is that I don't give up."

When Ronnie Goodman isn't painting, he runs. He runs up to fifty miles per week on the streets of San Francisco when training for a half-marathon, often wearing a Tamalpa Racing singlet from the local Tamalpa Runners running club. He's run a few half-marathons, including the San Francisco Half-Marathon in July of 2014, which he wanted to run for his birthday.

When you get to know Ronnie Goodman and talk to him about his experiences of being a runner, it doesn't take long to discover that his running and painting are intertwined. He speaks from his heart, yet is often nonchalant about things, brushing them off as if nothing special. "Running helps inspire me as an artist," he says. "When I get stuck creating a piece of work, running helps me step back from the canvas and helps me put ideas together. I can look at the canvas in my imagination."

Creative and imaginative thinking is arguably the pinnacle of cerebral function. It requires seeing things or ideas that are not already there. Many of us strive for it. There are lots of intelligent people with high IQs, who have memorization skills that rival those of a Broadway actor reciting a Shakespearean soliloquy. But to make those words come to life in a way that makes us believe that the actor is the character he or she is portraying, stirring something inside of us that makes us leave the theater different from how we entered it—those are the ones we look up to: the creative ones, who have original thoughts, who come up with ideas that leave us wondering how the heck they did it. Most people want to be more creative. I've met only a few people in my life who have said they're not creative and were perfectly fine with being that way.

As a writer and entrepreneur, my livelihood depends on my creativity. But creativity is more than just a living for me; it's a lifestyle. Being creative fulfills me on a deep level, whether I'm running, writing a book, speaking at a conference, or developing business ideas. There's something freeing about being creative, thinking on life's fringes, developing an idea and seeing it grow from concept to tangible product. But it's hard sometimes to think differently, to think outside of the box in which our educational system has put us. School doesn't teach us how to think. We're left to figure that out for ourselves.

I often come up with ideas while running. That may not seem very insightful. After all, ideas can come to us at any time of the day, sometimes even when we're sleeping. But there's something about running that enables those ideas to come to the surface, because they are much more difficult to come up with when I'm sitting at my desk and concentrating on them. The link between physical activity and creative thinking has caught the attention of more than one famous thinker. "The moment my legs begin to move my thoughts begin to flow," Henry David Thoreau said, "as if I had given vent to the stream at the lower end and consequently new fountains flowed into it at the upper." Through attaining a better physical self, we attain a more creative self.

While creativity is one of the most sought-after mental processes, it is perhaps the least understood. Science has linked creativity to mood, with positive moods generally improving creativity. A number of studies have shown that aerobic exercise—even a single session—significantly enhances mood and creative thinking, although it appears that the enhanced ability to think creatively is independent of any changes in mood, suggesting that creativity is not just a matter of mood.

Running seems to unlock our ability to think creatively. Research from Leiden University in the Netherlands has shown that people perform better on creative-thinking tests following a bout of aerobic exercise, compared to when the tests are taken without exercising first. The researchers also found that people who exercise score higher on creative-thinking tests than people who don't exercise. However, exercise only affects creative thinking if you're used to exercising. If you're not used to exercising, the mental effort that goes into the exercise itself detracts from the ability to think creatively after the workout is over, as if the workout itself is exhausting mentally as well as physically. It seems that exercising on a regular basis trains your brain to become more flexible in finding creative solutions, but only if your body is used to being active. Isn't that interesting— *only if your body is used to being active.*

Why does running on a regular basis enhance creativity? To answer this question, we need to understand what's happening when we're being creative, and for that, we need to look beyond our cardiovascular and muscular systems. Exercise doesn't just affect the heart and muscles; it also affects the brain. It's an interesting field of science called neuroplasticity—the ability of the brain to *change.*

Running causes morphological and neurochemical adaptations in the brain. It increases the volume of every region of your brain, including the frontal lobe, temporal lobe, parietal lobe, and hippocampus, and prevents the atrophy that often accompanies aging. Conversely, an inactive daily life is a risk factor for brain atrophy, specifically of the frontal lobe— the part of the brain responsible for emotions, problem solving, reasoning, and planning. Specifically, it affects your ability to recognize future consequences resulting from current actions, the choice between good and bad actions, the suppression of socially unacceptable responses, and your ability to determine similarities and differences between things or events. All of these factors are negatively affected by lack of exercise as you age and positively affected by staying or becoming active. Running also facilitates the interaction between the frontal lobe's prefrontal cortex and the amygdala. The prefrontal cortex is the part of the brain's frontal lobe that helps dampen the amygdala's fear and anxiety signals. With fewer constraints from fear and anxiety, we can think more clearly and freely.

If increasing the volume of your brain isn't enough to make you more creative, running does something even more spectacular to your brain. It causes *neurogenesis*—the formation of new neurons—in specific parts of the brain. Previously thought to occur only in the developing brain of a fetus and newborn, it's now accepted that neurogenesis occurs even in the mature brains of adults. The primary part of the brain where this neurogenesis occurs is the hippocampus, which is located under the cerebral cortex in the medial temporal lobe. The hippocampus is critically important for short-term and long-term memory, spatial navigation, and the regulation of emotions. Interestingly, it is one of the first regions of the brain to suffer damage in patients with Alzheimer's disease.

The hippocampus also contains high levels of glucocorticoid receptors, which makes it more vulnerable to long-term stress than most other areas of the brain. Studies have shown that animals that exercise undergo a sustained increase in neurogenesis in the hippocampus compared to animals that don't exercise. For example, when mice are given free access to a running wheel for a few months, they have more than twice the number of new cells formed in their brains compared to mice with no access to a running wheel.

Neurogenesis also means that running makes you smarter. Increased interactions between nerve cells means more parts of your brain can communicate with one another. And all this communication fosters what scientists call *divergent thinking*—what we call thinking outside of the box. A number of studies have shown that running improves fluid intelligence, including problem-solving ability, memory, learning, and pattern recognition. These improvements in cognitive function are even more observable as people age. Indeed, there is considerable evidence that lack of physical activity in the elderly is a risk factor for poor cognitive functioning. It seems that if you want to remain mentally sharp as you age, you had better run, or at least do some form of exercise. Physical activity triggers molecular and cellular changes that support and maintain brain plasticity. Studies have shown that physical activity sustains cerebral blood flow, increases nutrient supply to the brain, and facilitates neurotransmitter metabolism, all of which help you to think better.

It's likely that the relationship between physical activity and cognitive performance is reciprocal—increased physical activity leads to better cognitive functioning, and brighter people exercise more. I don't know that I run because I'm smart or that I'm smart because I run, but I know that running enables me to think in ways that I probably wouldn't if I didn't run.

Scientists in Hong Kong, China, and Canada wanted to find out how running causes the formation of new nerve cells in the hippocampus. Their research, which they performed on mice and was published in the *Proceedings of the National Academy of Sciences* in 2014, showed that this neurogenesis in the hippocampus is mediated by adiponectin, a protein hormone secreted by fat cells. Adiponectin modulates a number of metabolic processes, including glucose regulation in the blood and the oxidation of fat. It also possesses antidiabetic, anti-inflammatory, antiatherogenic, and cardioprotective properties. Adiponectin levels are inversely correlated with body-fat percentage in adults, which means that the lower your body-fat percentage, the higher your level of adiponectin. Running is a potent fat-burning activity, decreasing your body-fat percentage and thereby increasing the level of adiponectin. In other words, running may increase the formation of new nerve cells in your brain and make you feel good in large part because of the effect of decreasing your body-fat percentage. Now that's pretty cool.

It is the final of the Olympic 1,500 meters. "Runners, set," says the starter, as I take two steps forward and lean over the start line, the rectus femoris muscle in my quads flexing in anxious attention. After a quick start off the line, I settle into position, right behind the early leaders. I sit off their shoulders, stalking them like a lion stalking his prey, patiently waiting for the right moment to strike. And then, with 300 meters to go, I take the lead, and all I can think about is running as fast as I can away from everyone. I come off the final turn in the lead, and with 100 meters to go, I race toward the finish line, making the world chase me, but they can't, and I cross the line in pure bliss, an Olympic champion.

I cannot tell you how many times during a run this scenario has played like a video in my mind. I feel the experience as if it were really happening, my pace quickening at the thought. Running opens up our imagination, enabling us to see outside of our perceived limits. On a run, I am an Olympic champion. On a run, I can dream.

Unlike any other species, humans have a unique capacity—central to who we are as humans—to imagine ourselves different than we are, better than we are. We imagine a future for ourselves that does not yet exist. We imagine a life that we have never lived. We imagine a self we have never become. I may not have the raw talent it takes to fulfill my dream of becoming an Olympic champion, but my ability to imagine drives me to become a better runner and live a better life than I am now.

But this unique human capacity to imagine is not always full of rainbows and roses, offering us an opportunity for self-betterment. Imagining a self you have not become can also be as much a curse as it is a gift because you are always haunted by a sense and desire of wanting more, of regret that you have not fulfilled your potential of being human. For some, it can be paralyzing. It is up to us to choose whether our imagination will inspire us or haunt us.

Personally, I don't know that my runs are a way for me to be more creative. I don't have such a clear sense of how my running influences my writing or my other creative pursuits or my sense of self, like Ronnie Goodman does. I'm not sure if my post-run creativity is a result of forming new connections in my brain, my run's uplifting effect on my mood, or my low percentage of body fat, although I do notice that running is good for my mood. When I finish a run, everything is just a little bit better, my life and the way I look at the world. I get stirred up inside. Every day of our lives should have that inner stirring. And if I sit to write immediately after completing a run, the writing is often easier. There's a calmness that follows a run that, for this type-A personality, I can't get at any other time. Perhaps the creativity is already there, but somehow the calming effect of a run enables that creativity to come to the forefront. Running in different places, for different distances, and letting the thoughts come and go as they please helps this creative process. I love the feeling of my post-run shower, changing into dry clothes, and sitting in front of my computer to write in the post-run quiet and calm. Any runner who's in a bad mood knows that running is a great mood enhancer. Some swear it's even euphoric.

Indeed, you can't be a runner without hearing of the elusive runner's high. Much has been made of endorphins, those hormones released in response to aerobic exercise. Endorphins, runners say, make you feel euphoric, but I don't know that I buy that. In all my years of running, I don't ever recall feeling euphoric. I've never had that runner's high. Maybe I'm endorphin deficient. Is the runner's high real? And, if so, where's my share?

Various research studies have reported up to a five-fold increase in plasma beta-endorphin levels after exercise, and have often used this large increase as support of beta-endorphins being responsible for the runner's high. However, beta-endorphins are released into the bloodstream from the pituitary gland and can only marginally enter the brain through the blood-brain barrier. Thus, any existence of a runner's high, perceived or real, is not likely a result of beta-endorphins, as has been previously thought from measurements of beta-endorphins in the peripheral blood. Other studies have shown that running activates opioid and cannabinoid receptors, releasing these chemical compounds in the frontolimbic region of the brain after sustained moderate- or high-intensity aerobic exercise. There is a high correlation of opioids and cannabinoids to the perceived euphoria of runners. So it seems that a runner's high does, or at least can, exist, but it's due to opioids and cannabinoids in the brain rather than endorphins in the blood.

I may be opioid as well as endorphin deficient, because I've never felt euphoric during or immediately after a run. But I don't run for the euphoric interludes. However, at times during a run, the movements of my legs feel easier, and my energy level is higher. I've felt in those moments that my body knows, ahead of my brain, how to perform. Renowned psychologist Mihaly Csikszentmihalyi of the University of Chicago calls this experience *flow*, a relaxed state in which you forget about time and feel confident and in control. It's as if my body is breaking the first law of thermodynamics and actually creating energy. The energy creates nothing less than a learning experience, during which I can learn about my body and its world in a unique way. I spend the precious time learning about such things as thinking and being, association and solitude, reality and fiction. What is fiction to everyone else becomes my reality, just as the characters on the novel's page are real to its author. I'm the author of my body, feeling like I've just created and discovered movement as if for the first time.

The moment of flow, like most great moments in life, is fleeting, lasting only a mile or two during my run. Then I return to feeling normal, and the running once again becomes a conscious endeavor. The scientist in me wants to know what causes this feeling, this ease of movement, and why it only happens on certain occasions. Maybe it has something to do with the alignment of the moons. Maybe my Jupiter is not aligned with my Saturn this month. However, the philosopher and the athlete in me don't care at all about why this happens, only about the moment and the feeling. Perhaps someday the science will catch up to the anecdotal evidence. Perhaps I have endorphins and opioids after all.

Ronnie Goodman knows the human despair he paints about in The Gallery on Haight Street. Experiencing depression after his mother passed away, he tried to self-medicate with drugs, using marijuana, heroin, and cocaine. He spent eight years in San Quentin Prison for burglary. He's been homeless since 2000. He's got four kids, one of whom was stabbed to death. His ex-wife doesn't want anything to do with him since he became a drug addict. "Once you get into drugs, you lose everything," he says.

Sober since 2003, Ronnie lives a pretty simple life on the streets in San Francisco. He paints, and he runs. Even without having much to his name, he still gives back to the community that has supported his painting and running. He sells his prints, posters, greeting cards, and T-shirts in The Gallery and on his website. He manages the studio in exchange for painting in it. He donates his artwork to churches. And he fund-raises for Hospitality House, an organization that provides programs for San Francisco's homeless community.

Ronnie has been running on and off since elementary school. "I run completely for enjoyment," he says. He was competitive in junior high school, but he didn't get serious about running until much later in life, ironically when he was in prison. It was there that he met a volunteer named Frank. A runner himself, Frank started the 1,000 Miles Running Club in Ronnie's prison. Ronnie joined, saying he wanted to do something healthy for himself. While in prison, Ronnie ran four times per week for an hour to an hour and a half. Around a courtyard. He even ran four marathons in prison—105 laps around a quarter-mile track.

"Running gets you into a meditative mode," he says, with the philosophical perspective of the artist that he is. "It makes you see things differently. If I'm going through something that might have happened the day before that made me feel depressed, I put on my shoes and run, and it's like, 'Oh, it's a wrap, it's over with. I just ran, I feel good. I don't need to stick to those feelings that made me feel bad. I'm feeling good now, and I'm going to stick with that.'"

Since getting out of prison, he's run a few half-marathons and has even run the famous Dipsea Trail Race in Marin County, California, the oldest trail race in America. His half-marathon PR is 1:38, which he ran in his fifties.

When asked how he runs being homeless, he says, "I just do." There's little more to that answer. But I wanted to know the little more that there was, so I asked him the questions that most runners would want to know about a homeless runner.

"How do you take a shower?" I asked.

"I take a shower at community-resource centers in San Francisco."

"How do you eat?"

"I go to a local church to eat."

"How do you buy running shoes?"

"When I sell a piece of art, I use the money to buy running shoes."

I was curious about how I was able to interview this guy on the phone.

"There's a service called Homeless Connect Voicemail for homeless people," he told me, "in case any family members need to get in touch with someone who's homeless."

When you ask the former drug addict and ex-con *why* he runs, you get an answer that has *a lot* more to it. "When I'm running, I feel like I'm not there. I feel like I'm somewhere else. I feel like I'm inside of myself. It's like this spiritual moment that I'm just running and running. I might run for two hours, and I'm a free person for those two hours."

Sometimes Ronnie runs with his friend Frank, the prison volunteer who started the 1,000 Miles Running Club. But he often runs alone, using his runs to imagine and create the art that he'll paint later that day.

Some would look at Ronnie Goodman and feel sorry for him. But he doesn't feel sorry for himself. Quite the contrary.

In many ways, he's turned his life around, and he's living the life that he wants to live, painting and running and giving back to the community with his art. How many of us who have money and luxuries don't give back at all? How many of us are pursuing our deep passions? How many of us find true inspiration in the things we do and use running to open our minds and create art—whatever form that art may be? Ronnie does.

I finished my conversation with Ronnie by asking him what he wants people to know about him.

"I just want people to know I'm an artist and a runner. It makes me feel alive."

Running is the place where we *all* become artists, where we can dream and imagine and create the life we want for ourselves.

PRODUCTIVE RUNS

"THE MAIN THING IS TO KEEP THE MAIN THING THE MAIN THING."

I n Escondido, California, Kristin Stehly gets out of bed at 4:30 a.m. She brews some coffee and sleepwalks in the dark downstairs to her basement, nearly tripping over one of her hairless cats. She puts on the shoes and running clothes that wait for her next to the treadmill and runs ten to fifteen miles while she watches *The Devil Wears Prada* on Netflix.

"The majority of my running is in the early-morning hours on the treadmill, before anyone else is awake," she says. "Once the day starts, it's nonstop, so that's the only chance I get."

After about twenty minutes, she hops off the treadmill to stretch for a few seconds. Her hip is bothering her again. She was diagnosed with a degenerative hip condition as a kid that still gives her trouble with left hip dysplasia. She runs through it the best she can. A recent labrum tear prevented her from running at all. Her doctor says she'll probably need hip surgery at some point.

At 6:30 a.m., she jumps in the shower. She gets dressed, then wakes up her five-year-old twin sons, prepares their breakfast, and packs their lunches before taking them to school. Before leaving, she attends to the family's many pets, including three cats, two of which are hairless, and lots of birds and tortoises that roam the property around her house. Kristin and her husband, the lead bird keeper at San Diego's Safari Park, have a love for animals.

With kids in tow, she's out the door by 7:30 a.m. After dropping the kids off, she goes to her full-time job in nearby Valley Center as a middle-school physical-education teacher.

Like many moms who work full-time, Kristin is pretty busy. But unlike many moms, Kristin also runs half-marathons and marathons. A lot of them. She's run about thirty half-marathons and twenty-six marathons. In 2014 alone, she ran eight half-marathons and eleven marathons, and has PRs of 1:30 and 3:17. To train for these races, she runs fifty to sixty miles per week, most of them on the basement treadmill. She started running half-marathons when she was twenty-six.

"Running makes me more productive, because it helps me focus on my goals—not just my running goals, but also my life goals," she says. "I know I need to get things done when I have the chance to do them. Running motivates me in pretty much all other areas of my life."

She arrives back home between 3:30 and 4:00 p.m. A couple of days each week, she drives straight from school to the YMCA in Encinitas to teach either a KettleWorx class or a high-intensity, cardio-circuit class with plyometrics as a part-time group-fitness instructor. After class, she drives home to be with her family and cook dinner for her sons and husband.

"I'm all about finding easy, healthy meals to prepare quickly," she says. "I like to find the least complicated way to get things done efficiently."

As she's cooking dinner, she gives her kids a bath and gets them into their pajamas. After dinner, she cleans up the kitchen and reads to them.

"On a daily basis, I have to decide if I want to spend more time in the kitchen or get a run in," she says. "It's hard as a mom, because we put so much pressure on ourselves to be able to do it all, but the reality is that, if you're going to devote enough time to running, something else has to give. I don't really care if I show up to a party with the most elaborately wrapped gift or decadent dessert. I had to learn to not compare myself with others. Not everyone loves to run, so not everyone understands. It's my passion, though, and hopefully by living my passion, it inspires others to follow theirs."

When I was in high school, I attended a track camp. Sort of like band camp, but we ran instead of played instruments. The name of the camp was The Mighty Burner Speed Camp. It was a pretty unique camp, not just because of its name, which might sound intimidating to some, but because of the four camp coaches. They were the members of the United States' 1,600-meter relay team that competed at the 1968 Olympics in Mexico City. The four athletes who each ran a 400-meter leg of the relay were the fastest 400-meter runners of their generation—Vince Mathews, Ron Freeman, Larry James, and Lee Evans. Together at the Olympics, they won the gold medal in the 1,600-meter relay and set the world record of 2 minutes and 56.16 seconds, which stood for twenty years. Individually, Lee Evans won the 400-meter gold medal and set the world record of 43.86 seconds. Larry James, whose nickname was The

Mighty Burner, won the 400-meter silver medal and ran the second-fastest time in history of 43.97 seconds. Ron Freeman won the 400-meter bronze medal, running 44.41 seconds, which means that the US relay team had all three medalists in the open 400 meters. (The fourth member of the relay team, Vince Matthews, who placed fourth at the US Olympic Trials and so did not run the open 400 meters in Mexico City, won the 400-meter gold medal at the 1972 Olympics in Munich, Germany.) To say these guys were studs is an understatement.

A man of words as well as fast legs, Larry James had a saying for us impressionable high-school runners at his camp, which, I found out years later, he borrowed from psychologist and author Stephen Covey: "The main thing is to keep the main thing the main thing."

"What's the main thing?" he asked us, as we collected as a group on the track.

"The main thing is to keep the main thing the main thing," we responded in unison.

"What's the main thing?"

"The main thing is to keep the main thing the main thing."

"What's the main thing?"

"The main thing is to keep the main thing the main thing."

Running directs your efforts, helping you to keep the main thing the main thing. There's nothing like a long run to put the issues in our lives into perspective. We worry about things that don't happen; we waste our time on things that don't matter; we follow paths that lead to dead ends. Running puts us on the right path. It directs us toward a life of meaning. And it helps us get more done.

I see my day in two parts—the time I spend running and the rest of my day. When I know I *have* to run, I can always find the time to do it. Humans are driven by what they want to do and by what they feel they have to do. There is no compromise. And because I need to make time to run, I have to be better at organizing the rest of my day.

Every person I meet is quick to tell me how busy he or she is. "Busy" may be the most overused word in the dictionary, even though research (and TV-Nielsen ratings) shows that people have more leisure time than ever before. Being busy is not a worthwhile pursuit. Being productive is. What really matters is not how much you undertake, but what you actually accomplish. People know the names of the athletes on that Olympic 1,600-meter relay because of what they accomplished in Mexico City.

I have always believed it is better to do one thing very well than a number of things very averagely. Running gives us all a chance, regardless of the genes we were born with, to become better than average, to become productive, to become accomplished. When we keep the main thing the main thing, we are productive, rather than busy.

After all my years of running, I still feel like my productivity and my sense of accomplishment hinge on running over everything else. Even if I get nothing else done the rest of the day, I still feel like I accomplished something if I ran. I suspect many other runners feel the same way. Since I run every day, every day includes a sense of accomplishment. I walk back inside my front door after completing a run, thinking, "Check! I just placed one more piece of the puzzle in the picture to achieve my goal." It's the exact opposite feeling of training haphazardly, with no direction. As Yogi Berra said, "You've got to be very careful if you don't know where you're going, because you might not get there." Don't waste your time with runs that don't meet a specific purpose, even if that purpose is purely for the fun of it or to relieve stress. If you're going to put effort into something, isn't it better to have that effort be worth something, rather than be a waste of your time? When you have purpose, you become a stronger, better, more productive runner who feels like you can do anything.

Sport psychologists from here to Timbuktu have become notorious for telling athletes to set goals. And they're right—goals direct our efforts, leading us to specific outcomes and achievements. For athletes, studies show that goals affect everything from enhancing athletic skills to increasing weekly running distance. When we set goals, we change our behavior in an effort to achieve them. We become more productive, focusing on the things that will get us there and eliminating the things that won't.

Most people complain that they don't have time to exercise. Indeed, lack of time is the most common excuse for not exercising. But the amount of time that people perceive they would lose by exercising is more than made up for during the rest of the day. Running makes you more confident, more creative, more passionate, more energetic. As a result, you actually get *more* done the rest of the day, not less. Running has a way of playing with time, of enhancing your self-management.

Lack of time is really not much of an excuse when we consider how much of it we waste. I've noticed that people who have plenty of time on their hands don't get much done. It's too easy to waste time when you don't have a lot to do. How much time does the average person spend watching television or looking at and commenting on friends' Facebook and Instagram photos? How much time does the average person who wants to lose weight spend sitting on his or her couch reading weight-loss books? The US has a lot of weight-loss book readers but not enough weight losers. Running solves this problem.

One of the things I like about running is how much can be accomplished in a very short time. It doesn't take much running to see a large benefit. Most types of running workouts can be done in less than an hour. Go to your local track, warm up for one to two miles, run six to ten 400-meter reps (one lap) at a fast pace with an equal amount of time jogging for recovery between each rep, and cool down for a mile, and in less than an hour, you just accomplished one of the best fitness-boosting workouts you'll ever experience in your life. After a workout like that, it's hard not to feel like you did something good for yourself. It's hard not to take that feeling to everything else you do during the day.

There are plenty of anecdotes from CEOs and entrepreneurs that the confidence, motivation, creativity, and productivity derived from exercise drives success. Life is not just survival of the fittest, as Darwin argued; it is also success to the fittest. Take the research of Vasilios Kosteas, an economist at Cleveland State University, who studied whether exercising on a regular basis leads to earning more money in the labor market. He found that a sedentary individual who starts to exercise a few times per month will see an average of a 2.2 percent increase in his weekly earnings, an individual who exercises one to three times per month earns an average of 5.2 percent more than a sedentary individual, and individuals who exercise on a regular basis earn 6 to 9 percent more. Using sophisticated, statistical procedures to tease out the details of the relationship, he showed that regular exercisers and greater financial success are not just related—the relationship between the two is *causal*; that is, people who exercise earn more *because* they exercise. People who exercise, especially those who train in pursuit of a goal, are driven to be successful. Seventy-three percent of people who run regularly have a household income of more than $75,000, compared to the US median household income of $52,700.

Another study examined the relationship between academic achievement and physical fitness among elementary and middle-school children. Academic achievement was assessed as a passing score on the Massachusetts Comprehensive Assessment System achievement tests in mathematics and English. Fitness achievement was assessed as the number of physical-fitness tests that the students passed during physical-education classes. The researchers found that the odds of passing both the mathematics and English tests increased as the number of fitness tests the students passed increased, even when the researchers controlled for confounding factors that could affect either academic achievement or physical fitness—including body weight, ethnicity, sex, grade, and socioeconomic status. Even in cultures in which academic achievement is placed in high regard, such as in the competitive Chinese society of Taiwan, there is a strong link between physical-fitness test scores and students' academic achievement.

We see this trend in other environments as well. It's no coincidence that college cross-country teams tend to have among the highest GPAs of any athletic team on campus. The discipline, motivation, and volume of work it takes to be a good runner is parallel to what it takes to be a good student. If you want your kids to excel in school, tell them to run. Seventy-five percent of runners are college educated, compared to just 30 percent of the general US adult population.

When people find out that I'm a writer, many of them tell me they don't have the discipline to sit for hours at a time and write a book. I have a friend who writes a newsletter for his company that he sends to his clients, and he tells me that he has trouble sitting down for even an hour to write the newsletter. One of the ways that running makes you more productive is by teaching you discipline. It takes discipline to run every day. It takes discipline to write a book. Especially these days, when we are distracted by social media, e-mail, texts, home-shopping channels, reality TV, iTunes, smartphones, and the Kardashians, it's hard to focus on productive work. We have become a society of convenience and laziness. Running goes against the grain of modern society. But that's exactly why it teaches you discipline—because you have to put down the remote control and stop looking at your friend's Facebook pictures to run. The discipline you learn from running carries over to the rest of your life. Running distinguishes what's important in life from what is not. It puts into perspective, squarely and right in front of us, what really matters.

It's 8:00 p.m., time for Kristin Stehly to get her five-year-old twins ready for bed. At about 8:30 p.m., she sits down in front of her computer to write a blog post, complete with the pictures of her compression socks that she wore during her last half-marathon and the healthy snacks she ate throughout the day. Kristin is a brand ambassador for a number of athletic and nutrition companies. She writes about the products and her life as a runner and foodie on her popular blog at StuftMama.com. When she finishes posting her blog between 10:00 and 10:30 p.m., she goes to sleep.

Being a mom and a wife are her top priorities, but trying to fit in everything else with a full-time job, teaching fitness classes at the gym, blogging, and trying to get enough sleep is definitely a struggle. It's hard to get Kristin to sit down for an interview. To understand how she fits running into everything she does, we need to understand what drives people to make the choices they make.

One of the strongest motivators that makes people do something is that they *want* to do it. That's why, as Dale Carnegie says in his book, *How to Win Friends and Influence People*, to influence someone to do something, you need to arouse in the other person an eager desire to do it.

"If something is important to you, you make time for it," Kristin says. "I have to make the time to run. I found out a long time ago that I will never get more time, but if it's important to me, I'll make the time. Even if it's just a quick forty-minute window, if I get the chance to run, I take it."

But it's not always easy. And it's the not easy part that prevents millions of people from running when they're busy with work and family. While it oftentimes may seem selfish to those around us, because running takes time from things others may want us to immediately do for them, the benefits of being a runner accrue to those around us in a wide range of ways, from our ability to be good parents and spouses to mentoring and inspiring others.

"I run because it makes me a better mom, wife, friend, and teacher. It makes me a better person. I want to inspire others to believe in themselves and dream big. I started running later in life, and I really shouldn't be able to run given my hip disease, but I can and I do. I think running can make anyone a better person. It's about getting out there and getting out of your comfort zone and reaching new goals."

CONFIDENT RUNS

"IF I HAD NOT BEEN GIVEN THE GIFT OF SOMETHING SO ORDINARY, MY LIFE WOULD HAVE EVOLVED IN A COMPLETELY DIFFERENT AND MUCH MORE MUNDANE MANNER."

When you walk into the state-of-the-art Human Performance Laboratory on the campus of the University of Calgary, nestled in the shadows of the Canadian Rockies, you can't help but be in awe. Built in preparation for the 1988 Winter Olympics, it is one of Calgary's many Olympic legacies. The first thing you see when you walk through the laboratory's front double doors is five lanes of running space that span the length of the room. Force plates are built into the rubberized floor, and cameras on tripods surround the area. People run on the track, first with running shoes, then in bare feet—the force plates measuring how much force is applied at different parts of the foot under these conditions—and the cameras capture every angle of the runner's movements to create a three-dimensional picture that will be analyzed using motion-analysis software.

In another room, an athlete runs on a treadmill built into the tile floor while breathing through a snorkel-like mouthpiece. The mouthpiece is connected to a hose that is then connected to analyzers that measure the volume of both consumed oxygen and exhaled carbon dioxide. Every five minutes, as the athlete continues running, blood is drawn from a catheter in a vein in her arm to measure the concentration of lactate and other metabolites.

In a different part of the lab, the research quickly changes from whole-body movement to microscopic muscle. Dr. Walter Herzog, an imposingly tall, thin man and co-director of the Human Performance Laboratory, stands among some sophisticated equipment.

"We're identifying the molecular mechanisms of muscle contraction," he says in his Swiss German accent, as if it's just another day at the office.

Walter is one of the world's top scientists in the fascinating and wide-reaching field of biomechanics, which merges the physics and biology of human movement. His faculty position at the University of Calgary traverses a few departments, including kinesiology, engineering, and medicine. His main emphasis of research these days is on the neuro-biomechanics of skeletal muscle. His research is both experimental and theoretical in nature, and includes cell manipulation, mechanical testing, finite-element modeling, continuum mechanics, simulations, and theories of growth and adaptation of soft and hard tissues. Heavy stuff.

Most of what Walter does goes over my head. I understand only about every other sentence he says. One of his recent publications is titled, "Tibiofemoral Loss of Contact Area But No Changes in Peak Pressures After Meniscectomy in a Lapine *In Vivo* Quadriceps Force Transfer Model." To say he's a pretty smart guy would be an understatement.

For the past fifteen years, his research has focused on the role of molecular proteins in skeletal-muscle contraction, namely a protein called titin. To study titin and see how it interacts with the more popular muscle proteins of actin and myosin, he and his research team need to look at muscle on a molecular level, examining rod-like structures inside muscle fibers called myofibrils and even isolating the repeated sections that run the length of the myofibrils, called sarcomeres, the smallest units of muscle contraction. His lab was the first and, so far, only one of two labs in the world to isolate and mechanically test properties of isolated sarcomeres. His research is shedding new light on how the proteins inside muscles work together to cause muscle contraction.

In 2006, Walter won the prestigious Borelli Award, which, fittingly, is named after the seventeenth century scientist Giovanni Alphonso Borelli, whose book, *De Motu Animalium* (*Of Animal Motion*), is perhaps the oldest documentation of a scientific study of running. It's fitting, because Walter is not just a great scholar. He's also a lifelong runner. His favorite race is 800 meters, the metric equivalent of a half mile.

"Running twice around the track as fast as I can has fascinated me for many years," he says.

Now at age sixty, Walter has been running ever since he can remember. He grew up speaking German in Zurzach (later renamed Bad Zurzach), a town of two and a half square miles on the Rhein River in the northern part of Switzerland. His first race was at the age of six, when he competed in a 60-meter sprint race. He was the fastest kid in town, although he jokes that the town had only sixteen boys his age, so it wasn't that hard to be the fastest. But running for Walter wasn't just about being fast.

"From very early on as a kid, I realized that my bodily and spiritual well-being—my body and my brain—were one and the same and intricately connected."

Like many other kids growing up in Switzerland, most of the running he did was while playing soccer. He played competitive soccer from the age of six or seven and then entered local races—sprints, cross-country, and on the road.

"The first time I realized that I probably had a bit of talent for running was when I went to the Swiss Age-Group Championships at age twelve, and I won the 600-meter race and placed second in the high jump and long jump without any formal training, only with soccer games that lasted all Saturday afternoon," he says. "I probably ran ten to twenty kilometers (six to twelve miles) during those games."

At age fourteen, still playing soccer but without any formal run training, he competed again at the Swiss Age-Group Championships and placed fifth, while breaking three minutes in the 1,000-meter run, and placed third in both the shot put and long jump. At seventeen, he joined an official track club for the first time and ran 800 meters in 2:04. At eighteen, he ran 1:57, and at nineteen, he ran 1:52. Later that year, he and his two best friends won the 3x1,000-meter relay at the Swiss National Championships, setting the Swiss record that stood for many years.

When Walter turned twenty, his goal was to run 800 meters in 1:48, which was about four seconds off the world record at that time. Having run "only" 1:51, he decided to study full-time and forget about his international and Olympic ambitions. "I felt that I was a couple of seconds too slow to ever be competitive on the international level," he says.

He continued training three to five times per week, going on half-hour runs and a couple of track workouts each week in the summer, and continued to run 800 meters between 1:51 and 1:53 on moderate training until he was twenty-eight years old. Then he stopped running competitively. He cross-country skied throughout the winters and ran recreationally in the summers, but it would be twenty years until he would compete again on the track.

Imagine, for a moment, that it is 1932, and you are at the World Series between the Chicago Cubs and the New York Yankees at Wrigley Field in Chicago, and Babe Ruth is at the plate. The pitcher throws the ball to the catcher; the Babe swings his robust torso and misses. Strike one. The pitcher throws again. Babe swings, misses. Strike two. Before the next pitch, Babe does something that catches your attention and the attention of everyone in the stadium. He points his chubby finger toward center field. "What is he doing?" you ask yourself. But before you can answer, the next pitch is on its way to home plate. This time, Babe swings; the ball cracks off his heavy bat and sails over the center-field wall. Home run. You are astounded. "How did he do that?" you ask your friend sitting next to you. But he doesn't know. No one knows. Except for Babe Ruth.

The reason he was able to call his own home run was because he believed he could. He was confident in that situation. At that particular moment, facing that particular pitcher, Babe Ruth had a high level of confidence.

Being able to do extraordinary things isn't that uncommon. It just takes a certain amount of confidence in one's abilities. We are all capable of doing great things. We just don't often know or believe that.

But great things don't have to be the focus of our lives. For some people, just getting out the door to run for fifteen minutes is a worthy accomplishment. Great accomplishments and commonplace tasks both require a certain conviction that one can carry out the behavior required to produce a desired outcome. In the 1970s, psychologist Albert Bandura came up with a term to describe that conviction—*self-efficacy*, a situation-specific self-confidence. Bandura defined self-efficacy as people's judgments of their capabilities to organize and execute courses of action required to attain designated types of performances. It is concerned not with the skills one has nor one's ability per se, but with one's judgment or assessment of what one can do with one's abilities. When we believe, we do.

Creating these judgments begins, like most self-assessments, when we're very young. Initial efficacy experiences are centered in the family, but as our social world rapidly expands as kids, peers assume an increasingly important role in us developing self-knowledge of our capabilities.

Bandura's theory of self-efficacy has attracted many researchers' attention in the area of health and exercise psychology. It has been used to study, among other things, why people begin to exercise. Research has found that other motivators of exercise, like fear arousal—such as the risk of disease—have not encouraged people to start an exercise program with the same reliability as has self-efficacy. What people believe about their ability to accomplish something has consistently proven to be among the most important determinants of physical activity and sport behavior. People run because they believe they can. And people don't run because they believe they can't.

We are all insecure about something. It does not matter how big of a rock star you are, how much money you have, how beautiful or intelligent you are, or how talented of a runner you are. I have yet to meet someone who is not insecure about something. Find something that gives you self-acceptance.

Running strengthens our belief in ourselves and what we can do. It fills the hole created by insecurity. How many people do you know who run a marathon and then think they can do anything? How people feel about themselves and their capabilities is arguably the most important factor in determining what actions and directions people take in their lives. And it determines how successful they are. Research on athletes has shown that the higher their self-efficacy, the better they perform. Indeed, athletes use self-efficacy statements more than any other strategy when trying to psych themselves up for competition. We are not just what we think; we are what we think we are.

Running has always been my path to self-acceptance. Being a runner has always been who I think I am. Even though I never reached the level I wanted to with running, it has always been my way to feel good about myself. Let's face it—winning a race, any race, is good for the ego. But I know running is not for everyone. There are some people—let's call them crazy—who don't like to run. I know for you and me, it's hard to believe, but they are out there. No matter how eloquent I try to be in explaining the benefits of running, it still doesn't interest them. That's okay. We can't all be runners. Variety is the spice of life. Our differences are what make life—and people—interesting. Find something that you're best at, what you feel good doing, something that gives you confidence, something through which you feel self-acceptance.

The year after I completed my PhD, I was invited to present my dissertation research at the American College of Sports Medicine Annual Conference. It's an intimidating conference to go to as a graduate student, or even as a newly minted PhD, because in attendance are the top scientists in the world in the interdisciplinary field of exercise science—physiology, biomechanics, kinesiology, physical therapy, motor learning, sport psychology, anatomy, biochemistry, and medicine. Being around these researchers, I was more than a bit nervous. I'll let you in on a little secret—I have always been a little worried that, in the right environment with people who are smarter than me, they will see right through me. This may be my twin brother's fault. After all these years, he still thinks he's the smarter twin, and he may be right. I've always had to work hard to get good grades. For my brother, school came easy. So I was nervous about presenting my research at this conference, where there would be many people who could embarrass me if they wanted to.

Many of the research presentations at this conference are given in themed sessions, so attendees can choose which theme they want to see. My dissertation, which was on the coordination of breathing and stride rate in runners, was placed in the theme of respiratory physiology. While writing my dissertation, I became intimately familiar with the research of the top respiratory exercise physiologists, so I knew who might show up.

I sat in the room with the other conference attendees, waiting for my turn to speak. For one of the presentations, a scientist presented his research that contradicted the findings of Dr. Jerry Dempsey of the University of Wisconsin, whose research on respiratory physiology and exercise is known all over the world. After this scientist finished his presentation, someone from the back of the room spoke. I turned my head, and it was Jerry Dempsey. Let's just say the next few minutes were a bit heated. Like a territorial tiger defending her cub, Dr. Dempsey called the other scientist out, blatantly told him that his research was garbage and his findings were wrong, and defended his own work. It wasn't pretty to watch. In fact, it got so heated that I could see it was making others in the room feel uncomfortable. Including me. Guess who was the next presenter?

After about five minutes of this back-and-forth diatribe about the other's research, it was my turn to give my presentation. At first, I thought, "I have to follow that?" A lot of things go through your head during a moment like this. It was easy to get distracted by the argument. Do I let my nerves get the best of me? I was already nervous about people like Jerry Dempsey in the room. I had read his research. He had a lot more experience in this subject area than I had.

The moderator of the session said, "The next presentation is *Lungs and Legs: Entrainment of Breathing to Locomotion in Highly Trained Distance Runners* by Jason Karp." That was all I needed to hear. I got up out of my seat, went to the front of the room, stood at the pulpit ready to show my first PowerPoint slide, and I did what any other confident runner would do—I cracked a joke about what had just happened. It got a laugh from the audience, and then I started my presentation. After I had finished, I was asked only a few soft questions about my research, and Jerry Dempsey didn't say a word. I walked out of the room and breathed a sigh of relief.

When I'm in a situation like this, I always fall back to running. I see myself as a runner first. Running, and especially racing, teaches you composure. There are lots of things that can happen during a race that can take you out of your game plan. Some of those things may have nothing to do with the race itself. It may be raining. You may have eaten too much pasta the night before. A relative may have recently died. Some of the distracting things may be directly related to the race. Runners may be better than you, or they may start the race at too fast of a pace, or they may box you in when you race on the track, or you may get stuck behind a large crowd in a road race with little room to run your pace. Your training may not have gone the way you liked leading up to the race. You may have a cold. You may even feel in the middle of a race like you have to take the biggest dump you've ever had to take. It happens. But whatever happens, you have to maintain your composure and focus on the task in front of you to earn the outcome you want. You have to focus on the reason you woke up early that morning and went to the starting line. That's part of being an athlete. That's part of being the better person you're aiming, through running, to be. Running provides the optimal forum in which to practice composure so that when you are away from the track or the road and in a convention center about to give a presentation in front of a room full of scientists with big egos, you can crack a joke, put everyone at ease, and nail your presentation.

If you stand at the finish line of a big race, you'll notice the expression on runners' faces, the raised arms, the fists pumping in the air as they cross the finish line. There is a true sense of accomplishment and empowerment, whether a runner is finishing his or her first marathon or running a personal-best time. The feeling of empowerment isn't experienced only by the sedentary individual who decides to get up off his or her couch and train for a race. Even the world's best runners experience it. Steve Prefontaine, who held the American record in seven different track events—from the 2,000 meters to the 10,000 meters—before his death at the young age of twenty-four, once remarked, "A lot of people run a race to see who is fastest. I run to see who has the most guts, who can punish himself into exhausting pace, and then at the end, punish himself even more."

What is to be learned from all this punishment? Why do runners willingly inflict this discomfort upon themselves? Are we masochists who take pleasure in pain? Some runners, like Steve Prefontaine, are indeed of the masochistic variety, in that they truly get pleasure from the pain they feel during a hard workout or race. I admit, during some workouts, I push myself just a little harder to test the limits of what I can handle. I internalize the pain, try to thrive on it, and let the effort be its own reward. It's not easy to do this. It goes against the human nature to preserve our comfort. We like to be comfortable. But I do it anyway.

Most of us, on some level, think the pain is good for us. Somehow we think that the discipline and willpower to never quit, the willingness to give the effort of everything we have, leads to self-empowerment. If you can get through the difficult, and at times painful, runs and races, it empowers you, and that empowerment carries over to every aspect of your life. We rise above the pain, in running and in life. When you believe that you can accomplish anything, that is true personal freedom. You are no longer timid or scared of pursuing something, because your running has empowered you to be bolder. "When you achieve your dreams," Henry David Thoreau said, "it's not so much what you get, it's who you have become in achieving them."

The vision statement of Girls on the Run, an organization that promotes the value of running among school-age girls, states, "We envision a world where every girl knows and activates her limitless potential and is free to boldly pursue her dreams."

Girls on the Run was established in 1996 in Charlotte, North Carolina. The program provides preadolescent girls with the necessary tools to embrace their individual strengths and successfully navigate life experiences. With the help of over 120,000 volunteers, the Girls on the Run program serves over 150,000 girls in more than two hundred cities across North

America each year. In 2013, Girls on the Run hosted 258 5K events across the United States and Canada.

With twice-weekly meetings in teams of eight to twenty, the Girls on the Run program teaches life skills through dynamic, interactive lessons and running games. The twenty-four-lesson curriculum is taught by certified coaches and includes three parts—understanding themselves, valuing relationships and teamwork, and understanding how they connect with and shape the world at large. Running is used to inspire and motivate girls, encourage lifelong health and fitness, and build confidence through accomplishment. Important social, psychological, and physical skills and abilities are developed and reinforced throughout the program. At each season's conclusion, the girls and their running buddies complete a 5K, which gives them a tangible sense of achievement, as well as a framework for setting and achieving life goals. The result? Making the seemingly impossible possible, and teaching girls that they can.

We all have problems. No one gets through life without a few scratches, a few bumps, and a few bruises. Some of us have major catastrophes and crises. We worry incessantly about our health and our money and our children, and it never stops. Some use religion as a way to cope with life's problems. They go to church or temple or a mosque and pray to a higher power to make things better, to bear the burden that we cannot handle ourselves. Others turn to running as a form of religion, as their opportunity to reflect and talk to God. Running eliminates the stress of most of life's problems, heightening the enjoyment of the good things in life, at least for the precious moments that we run. We can literally put space between ourselves and our problems, inserting clarity in the space and developing the confidence to handle and deal with what is asked of us. If we're lucky and have learned how to transfer the skills, the confidence and empowerment that running gives us can make every hour of our lives better.

In a life over which we don't have a lot of control, running gives us control. *You* can decide to run. *You* can decide not to run. *You* can decide how far to run or how fast to run or how often or where or when to run. Running puts the control in *your* hands. Running gives you the confidence to take risks, to take the road that Frost reminds us will make all the difference in your life.

I first met Walter, whom I called Dr. Herzog, when he was forty years old. I was a twenty-two-year-old, inexperienced but overconfident master's degree student when I stepped into his office at the University of Calgary. I was both impressed and intimidated. I could tell he meant business. He revealed in a later conversation that he did not feel the same way about me and, in so many words, told me that his first impression of me was not good. It would take me the better portion of two years to change my academic advisor's opinion of me.

One day, I was sitting in Walter's office talking to him about the research project we were working on—the esoteric topic of muscle-fiber recruitment patterns during eccentric contractions—and I asked him where his ability came from to develop his own ideas about how and why muscles work the way they do. Anticipating he was going to say something like, "That's why I'm the advisor, and you're the student," I was surprised when he said, without hesitation, "Years of research." It wasn't until years later, after I had experienced years of research myself while working on my own PhD, that I understood what he had meant and had reached the empowering point where I could develop my own ideas.

After starting to compete again on the track at age forty-eight, Walter competed in the Masters World Track and Field Championships in Edmonton, Alberta, at age fifty "just because it was close by," he says. He placed third in the 400 meters and second in the 800 meters, running a quick 2:09 and losing by just one hundredth of a second. He currently holds several age-group records in Alberta in the 600 and 800 meters.

Now sixty, Walter still hopes to break 60 seconds in the 400 meters and run faster than 2:20 in the 800 meters. "Running 2:20 still feels like running 1:51 when I was young. It's the same effort, feels like the same speed, and still gives me the same satisfaction as when I was twenty years old."

Being a scientist and runner myself, I couldn't help but ask him how he sees running through the eyes of a scientist, especially one who has devoted much of his career to the mechanics of muscles.

"When I cross-country ski, I think a lot of the mechanics of it, because it is so technical that after fifty years of doing it, I am still getting better technically every year. When running, I never think about the mechanics or the muscles; running is just natural locomotion."

Walter is not just a scientist who runs fast for his age, although that alone would be interesting. Being a speedy scientist is central to who Walter is, because he wouldn't be a scientist at all if he didn't run fast.

"Having been given a bit of talent for running, it gave me the confidence for a life that I would never have found in my farming and working-class family," he says. "It opened doors and avenues that I would never have dared to explore otherwise. The fact is, if I had not been given the gift of something so ordinary, my life would have evolved in a completely different and much more mundane manner, because I would never have believed that a little kid from a little town could ever aspire to more than an ordinary working life in a small village. Running gave me confidence that I could not find anywhere else in my life. Without it, I would never have studied at university, and I would never have become an academic and a scientist. I would have become a laborer like my father, married to a local girl and happy with a little family."

A self-described quiet and calm person, Walter admits he wasn't nervous getting married, taking his PhD exams, being at the birth of his children, or anything else that he can think of. However, when stepping to the start line of an 800-meter race, everything changes. "I can barely control my muscles twitching, and my mind goes wild," he says. "It has been, by far, the most emotional thing I have ever done in my life. It is hard to understand, because running has no existential meaning, nor does it have any value. Nevertheless, it has had an emotional grip on me from when I was young that nothing else ever has."

And therein lies perhaps the greatest paradox of running: In something so inconsequential, that has no existential meaning, we find something so meaningful, something so profound, that it gives a six-year-old kid in a tiny farming village in Switzerland the confidence to go to another country to earn a PhD and become one of the top scientists in his field in the world.

BECOMING A BETTER RUNNER AND A BETTER YOU

"AND THE SHOULDERS TURNED OUT TO BE MY OWN."

Exit 8 off the New Jersey Turnpike puts you in the suburban town of Hightstown in New Jersey's Mercer County, ten miles southeast of Princeton University. Driving along South Main Street in Hightstown, you run into the campus of the Peddie School, a 500-student private, boarding high school perhaps best known for its rigorous academic standards and most famous graduate, Walter Annenberg, the former United States Ambassador to the United Kingdom and publisher and founder of numerous print and television media outlets.

If you take a walk around the beautifully manicured 280-acre campus of the Peddie School, which looks more like a college than a high school, you'll quickly learn that there is a cult on campus. In the winter, a bunch of students with no body hair walk around the school wearing long blue-and-gold hooded coats and smelling like chlorine. They are members of the swim team, the third thing for which Peddie is known.

At the east end of the Peddie School campus sits the indoor, state-of-the-art natatorium, where you'll find these swimmers spending countless hours, both before and after school, swimming back and forth, with the sole purpose of becoming the very best swimmers they can be. And at Peddie, the very best they can be means the very best in the country.

I attended Peddie for my junior year of high school, although I had little to do with the swim team. I'm not much of a swimmer. But the swimmers were hard to miss on campus, with their hooded varsity swim jackets and the buzz that always swirled around them. In my calculus class, I sat next to Barbara Jane (Bedford) Miller, a short-haired, gregarious blonde who goes by B.J., who set the national high-school record in the 100-yard backstroke and became an Olympic gold medalist. In my psychology class, I sat next to Nelson Diebel who, just two years later, would win the gold medal in the 100-meter breaststroke at the Olympics in Barcelona. As a team, Peddie has been ranked number one in the country eight times by *Swimming World* magazine, winning the so-called Mythical National Championships. Since 1992, the Peddie swim team has been represented at every Olympic Games.

Before important swim meets, you could overhear amusing discussions in the hallways about shaving down and tapering in an attempt to swim faster. As a member of the cross-country and track teams, I was also interested in getting faster. So I couldn't help but eavesdrop. "What are these odd-sounding things?" I wondered. "Could they work for me, too? Do swimmers have a secret?" What can runners learn from swimmers?

Most people, when they find out about my running background and what I do for a living, say to me, "Oh, I hate running," or,

"Oh, I can't run," or my personal favorite, "I'm not a runner," as if running is something reserved only for those skinny people with no body fat who can seemingly eat whatever and however much they want, wear running shoes with jeans in public, and have strong knees that somehow magically hold up to all that pounding.

A lot of people tell me they think running is boring, that it's too monotonous. I guess they're right about the monotony. There's not much to take your attention away from the physicality of what you're doing. Unless you run with someone else, there's no one to talk to, no ball or racket or any other piece of equipment, and you finish in the same place you start. You put one foot in front of the other, over and over and over again. Running is quite repetitive. It's a constant, cyclic movement of the legs and arms. This is especially true if you run on a treadmill. You get locked into a zone, and the movements become automatic. Even when running outside, you can get so lost in the movement that it's almost meditative. Some people love that meditation, but others don't.

Believe it or not, a lot of people hate running. Yes, it's true. Most people who hate to run don't stick with it for long enough to not hate it anymore. They never get past the difficulty of it. They quit before getting to the point that the effort becomes effortless. And therein lies the problem with running—because it is difficult at first and boring to many people, people avoid it and, consequently, never get to experience all the benefits it confers.

A lot of people tell me they've tried to run, but then they stopped because their knees hurt. People want to believe they can't do something simply because it's hard. But running is actually not very hard. It's a very natural activity. We all do it as toddlers without ever having to be taught how. Running is more natural than other human activities, like swimming or cycling or driving. Take a toddler to the park, and he's already running before you even tell him to run. Take a toddler to the pool, and he has no idea what to do.

Certain pathologies aside, most people can run if they learn how and practice. But it's hard for people. As natural a human movement as running is, it's still hard for most people who don't grow up doing it. It's harder than cycling, and it's harder than swimming. But, guess what? Life is hard. Just because running is hard doesn't mean you should shy away from it, any more than you should shy away from the hard parts of life. The trick is learning how to deal with the hard parts, so you can enjoy the fun parts. It is precisely in working through the difficulty that we reap the benefits that count the most. You really *can* run. And you really can run more than you do now. Is it going to be difficult? Probably. Is it going to be worth it? You bet it is. There are many ways to lower your cholesterol and blood pressure or get a sculpted butt; you don't *need* to run for that. But running gives you those things and so much more.

Humans evolved to run, especially long distances. Science has well documented that physical activity was a necessary part of early humans' lives; there was no other way to get food. Although humans fare rather poorly compared to other animals when it comes to all-out sprinting (the fastest speed for a human is 23.3 miles per hour—Usain Bolt's world records of 9.58 seconds for 100 meters and 19.19 seconds for 200 meters—compared to the nearly 70 miles per hour achieved by a cheetah), they are among the best long-distance runners. There are a number of reasons why.

Multiple human lineages, including that leading to *Homo sapiens*, evolved in African highlands at altitudes of 3,300 to 6,600 feet (1,000 to 2,000 meters). Thus, Darwin's natural selection would have favored those with enhanced aerobic abilities to tolerate the lower-oxygen environment of altitude. It's not surprising that the physiological traits underlying modern humans' tolerance to altitude are similar to those associated with greater endurance performance. The evolution of our physiology was inherently very dependent on efficient oxygen delivery and the development of oxygen-using aerobic metabolism, with a relatively minor dependence on anaerobic (oxygen-independent) metabolism. We needed oxygen to survive as a species.

Our lungs, which have an extremely thin, yet immensely strong wall over an enormous area, have evolved to be the perfect medium for the exchange of oxygen and carbon dioxide gases. Humans, along with other mammals and birds, are the only species to have a complete separation of pulmonary and systemic (whole-body) circulations, which is essential to protect the blood-gas barrier from the high vascular pressures that occur during exercise.

Our lungs are not the only reason why we're such good runners. The arch on the bottom of our foot has evolved to perform better than the most well-made suspension bridge, absorbing shock with each footfall. Our strong and thick Achilles tendon, named after the Greek hero of the Trojan War, acts like a perfect spring, converting elastic energy to kinetic energy to propel us forward with each step, like the snap of a tight rubber band.

But, perhaps most importantly, unlike other mammals, humans can sweat. A lot. With 2,000,000 to 4,000,000 sweat glands and the ability to sweat in excess of a gallon per hour, we have an excellent mechanism to regulate body temperature through evaporative cooling, thereby preventing ourselves from overheating from continuous muscular work. If you measure your skin temperature while you run, you'll find that it actually gets cooler, not warmer as one would expect. Combined with our many sweat glands, we have less body hair than our ancestors, which increases cooling through the convection of air over our skin. We can dissipate body heat faster than any other large mammal. Our ability to run long distances—and run down faster but less-enduring animals to death—enabled our early ancestors to provide food for their families and thrive as a species. Not only are humans born to run, we run to be born.

Lessons

I have a friend who has a son, Billy, who was born without a right arm. When Billy was born, his mother was very worried. She knew that life would be difficult for him. But she promised herself that she would try to give Billy as normal a childhood as possible. She didn't want to hold him back because of a disability and didn't want him to be viewed as having one.

When Billy was seven years old, he asked his mother if he could take karate lessons. At first, his mother was nervous at the idea. After all, karate can be very dangerous, especially for someone missing a right arm. But she remembered the promise she made to herself when he was born, so she agreed, hoping that Billy would be okay.

The first day of karate class, Billy met his sensei, who taught him a move and had him practice it. At the end of the first class, he sent Billy home and told him to come back next week. The next week, the sensei showed Billy the same move and had Billy practice it. Billy practiced the move again the following week, and the week after that, and the week after that. After a couple of months of lessons, the sensei said to him, "Billy, you are ready for your first karate tournament." Billy couldn't believe his ears.

"What?" he said, startled at the idea. "How can I be ready to compete? You've taught me only one move, and I don't have a right arm."

"Don't worry. You're ready," the sensei said confidently. Billy was so nervous that he didn't tell his friends at school; he didn't even tell his mother. He went alone with the sensei to the karate tournament. In his first match of the tournament, Billy nervously stood on the mat, facing his opponent. He didn't know what the heck to do. He had never been in this position before. He looked over to the sensei, shrugged his shoulders, and asked, "What do I do?" The sensei looked right at him and replied, "Do the move." So, Billy did the move, and he won the match. For his second match, again he was nervous. He stood on the mat, facing his opponent. Again, he looked over to the sensei, shrugged his shoulders, and asked, "What do I do?" The sensei replied, "Do the move."

So, Billy did the move, and he won the match. For his third match, again he was nervous, albeit a bit more confident than he was before. He stood on the mat, facing his opponent. Again, unsure of what to do against his stronger, more experienced opponent, he looked over to the sensei and asked, "What do I do?" The sensei replied, "Do the move."

So, Billy did the move, and he won the match. Billy did the move, the only one he knew, a few more times, winning each of his matches, until he made it to the finals. With each round of the tournament, he gained confidence. For the final championship match against the defending champion, Billy stood on the mat, facing his opponent. This time, he looked over to the sensei, but no words needed to be spoken. Billy nodded his head. The sensei nodded his head. Billy did the move, and he won the championship match. The crowd was on its feet. Billy was ecstatic. He had never accomplished anything like this before.

During the drive home with the tournament trophy in his hands, Billy said to the sensei, "Sensei, I don't understand. How was I able to win the karate tournament? I only know one—" The sensei stopped him before he could finish the sentence.

"Billy," he said authoritatively, "you have mastered the most difficult move in karate. There is only one defense for that move. For your opponent to defend that move, he would have to grab your right arm."

Becoming a better runner is, first, learning the right lessons, and, second, executing them. One of those lessons is to run more. It's one of the first things I tell people to do when they ask me how to get better, no matter what level of runner they are. For nearly all runners, it's the surest way to become better. That doesn't mean you have to quit your job and give your kids up for adoption so you can run 100 or more miles per week, like the best runners in the world do. For most people, increasing their current running mileage will give them a large return on their investment. How much running you do each week has the single biggest impact on your fitness, how fast you run, and how much you can control your races, if and when you run them.

Running more, even when those miles are completed slowly, makes you a faster, stronger, and better runner. Sounds counterintuitive. How does running more *slow* miles make you run *faster* and more *in control*? Well, that's because running lots of miles enhances many of the internal characteristics you need for good endurance. Most people think of endurance as the ability to run *longer*. But endurance is really the ability to *sustain a faster pace*. Most people have the speed to run fast for a short period of time. We all sprinted across the playground as kids. What's lacking is the ability to endure that pace over the whole duration of the race. What can be improved is our ability to sustain our efforts over the duration of our lives.

As runners, we tend to think a lot about how much we run. Indeed, the number of miles we run each week often defines our status. The more miles we run, the more we're validated—the more we think of ourselves as runners. Even other runners will ask you how much mileage you run and make judgments about you based on your answer. However, the amount of time spent running is more important than the number of miles, since it's the duration of effort (time spent running) that our bodies sense. A faster runner will cover the same amount of distance in less time than a slower runner or, to put it another way, will cover more miles in the same amount of time. For example, a runner who averages a 7-minute mile pace for 40 miles per week is running the same amount of time as a runner who averages a 10-minute mile pace for 28 miles per week (280 minutes per week), and therefore is experiencing the same amount of stress. And that's what matters—the stress. The slower runner may be running fewer miles, but the time spent running—and therefore the stimulus for adaptation—is the same. If a slower runner tries to run as much as a faster runner, the slower runner will experience more stress and therefore puts himself or herself at a greater risk for injury. We don't have to rush through life at someone else's pace; we have only to take life at the pace that is right for us.

Endurance is improved not by running a specific distance, but by running for a specific amount of time. The duration of effort is one of the key factors that arouse the biological signal to elicit adaptations that will ultimately lead to improvements in performance. Focusing on time rather than on distance is a better method for equating the amount of stress between runners of different abilities. Your legs have no comprehension of what one mile is or what 26.2 miles are; they only know how hard they're working and how long they're working. Effort over time.

Unless you're training all-out speed like Olympic gold-medal sprinter Usain Bolt, whose muscles need to be powerful to produce a lot of force in a very short period of time, you don't train to practice running faster. As a distance runner, you should train to enhance the physiological characteristics that enable you to run faster in the future. This is a different way to think about your training, but it's a way that will make you a better runner. Think of an assembly line: If you want to make more products, the better strategy is to increase the number of workers (physiological characteristics), so you have more assembly lines to do the work, rather than increase the speed at which the assembly-line workers perform. The goal of training is to obtain the greatest benefit while incurring the least amount of stress, so run as slow as you can to obtain the desired outcome. The best training method is the one that caters to who you are—physically, psychologically, emotionally. So you need to know yourself.

What are your strengths and weaknesses as a runner? Do you have better endurance or better speed? Which types of workouts seem easier for you, and which seem harder? Which types of runs do you get excited about? Are you able to hang with other runners during the middle stages of races, but get out-kicked before the finish line? Do you have a hard time maintaining the pace during the middle stages, but can finish fast and out-kick other runners? Do you have a good sense of pace? Are you impatient? Do you get overly nervous or anxious before races? How good is your finishing kick, and how far from the finish line can you sustain it? Do you run for enjoyment, for the thrill of competition, or to push yourself to your limits?

When you know yourself and your strengths and weaknesses, you can use those strengths and weaknesses to your advantage to become a better runner and run better races. For example, if you have great endurance, skew your training toward higher mileage and tempo runs. If you have great speed, skew your training toward faster interval workouts. If you've got a great sense of pace, run longer workouts and races in which proper pacing really matters. To be better at running—and everything else you do—know what you're good at, and focus your efforts on whatever that is. Just like my friend's son, Billy.

Commitment

There are many physiological and biochemical reasons for how and why you become a better runner that are all very interesting, and knowing them enables you to affect specific outcomes from your training and become more proficient at the task. But becoming a better runner isn't just about your heart and muscles and the rest of your physiology and biochemistry. It's also about *commitment*. Becoming good at running—at anything for that matter—requires practice and patience. Practice, because it takes repetition of a task to master it, and patience, because when we run we are trying to change things at the level of the cell. We are changing our chemistry, and that's a slow process.

The commitment you make to run every day, or at least multiple times per week, creates a habit inside of you. It transforms running from a hobby to something of *significance*. When you make something significant in your life, you can't help but get better at it and enjoy it more.

There's more to the commitment of running than just becoming a better runner, although for most runners, that would be enough. When you dig deeper, there is something even more valuable than shaving seconds off your 5K time or minutes off your marathon time. When you run more, you learn about yourself. You learn the effort it takes. You learn the grind. You learn what it means to do more, to be more, to be so fatigued that all you want to do is sleep. No matter what level of runner you are, devoting yourself to the journey of becoming a better runner strips you of the unnecessary baggage you clutter your life with. There's no time for reality television when you're on a mission. The journey forces you to shut up, stop complaining, and stop making excuses for why you can't do it. An important lesson of running is that it teaches you how to give more of yourself. And you come out the other end of the work a stronger, more confident, more capable person, knowing that when the going gets tough, the tough inside of you really *can* get going.

Sometimes, I just want to leave everything and everyone behind and be by myself, in some remote place with no distraction or temptation, and completely and wholeheartedly throw myself into an endeavor, without reservation or guilt or fear of failure. Because that's where the real lessons are. Do you ever want to do that yourself? Do you ever wonder what the results might be if you did? I've thought about going to hide out somewhere, in a cabin in the middle of the woods, and do nothing other than write and run: 10,000 words and 100 miles per week. I wonder what kind of writer and runner and person I'd become if I did that.

Committing to running creates a habit, not only of running, but of all the traits that it takes to be successful in all areas of your life, including discipline, devotion, and attitude. It takes a lot of discipline and devotion to get out the door to run, despite the weather or your mood or your kids or your busy schedule. And then do it again tomorrow. And tomorrow. And tomorrow. When you develop those traits, you can apply them to any other area of your life—your job, your family, your relationships. When you throw yourself into running fully and clear of the doubts that hold you back, the payoff is extraordinary, no matter what the time reads on your stopwatch.

When you put your heart into running, you don't just grow your heart structurally; you grow it metaphorically. When you put your heart into running for the sake of the emotional investment, your heart grows. There's tremendous value in that. Make a better heart, and you make a better person. In running, as in life, it is only when we make an emotional investment that we experience great reward. Running becomes meaningful. You begin to care more about your performance as a runner and as a person. If you've ever committed physically and emotionally to training, you know what I'm talking about. Just as running makes your muscle fibers more resilient to fatigue and increases their ability to endure a faster pace, so too does it increase your physical and psychological ability to endure.

Focus

On a recent 10-mile run, I thought about distractions. Life is full of distractions that divert our attention away from what we're doing and what we want to accomplish. Most situations that come up during the day are distractions. Even as I sit writing this paragraph in a coffee shop after my run, there are a number of distractions that can take me away from the writing—a conversation at the table behind me, an attractive woman reading *The Alchemist* in front of me, a crying baby a few feet away, a text coming through on my phone. They all mix together to take my thoughts away from what I'm doing. Then there are the distractions that require some action on our part. Those are the ones that really divert our attention and take up time. The errands we have to run, the family dinner we need to prepare, the long line we have to wait on at the DMV. We get caught up in so many minutiae that at the end of the day we don't have much to show for our efforts.

We lose focus. Most of us have goals, even if we are reluctant to say them out loud, but we lack or lose the focus to attain them. One of the reasons why people don't do what they want to get done is that they spend too much time attending to what they perceive as being urgent, even when it's actually not a high priority. Too much time is wasted performing tasks that don't lead to results. Urgent matters tend to take precedence over important ones. This is not effective, results-oriented behavior. If you have a real sense of purpose and understand what's really important to you, you'll soon find out that you won't have problems fitting everything into your schedule. Recognize the distractions in your life, what is urgent versus what is important, and work on limiting the distractions, so you can accomplish what you want.

When I run, I feel focused. Perhaps it's because there are no distractions that stop me from running. Regardless of what happens around me or the errands I have to do that day, one foot keeps following the other. I'm not going to stop. Committing to being a better runner and the daily training that accompanies that goal teaches you focus. Running has taught me all the focus I need to be successful in other areas of my life. And it can teach you, too. Don't worry about tomorrow. Tomorrow comes tomorrow. Focus on each day, and do today what you can do today. When you run, your efforts are directed into something productive. Every stride moves you closer to what you want to accomplish. I feel that if I don't get anything else done that day, at least I ran. And that's got to be worth something.

People often say, "Everything happens for a reason," or "When one door closes another opens," or "It wasn't meant to be," or some other version of the same idea. I wonder if that's all really true or if humans say things like that as a coping mechanism to feel better when bad things happen or in response to failure and rejection. Does everything really happen for a reason, or are some things just random? Do things happen because someone else made a choice? When people make a choice that is different from the one you want them to make, resulting in you not getting what you want, do you say that it wasn't meant to be as a way to cope with the disappointment? Do humans try to convince themselves of something that may not be true?

One of the things running has taught me is that we have control over some things, but not all things. We have control over whether or not we lace up our shoes and run out the door, and we have control over how many miles we run before we get back to the door. We have control, albeit sometimes just slight, to follow a runner next to us in a race when he or she picks up the pace. We have control over our training to become better runners. But we don't have control over many illnesses or injuries that take running away from us. We don't have control over the limit of our running performance that depends on our DNA.

Part of being a runner is the ability to let go of the things you can't control and focus on the things you can. The truth is that we don't really know if something is meant to be or not. There is no way for us to know. But running has a way of centering us, of keeping us focused, of getting down to the bottom of what really matters.

Effort

For many people, running seems silly. You put one foot in front of the other and run until you don't feel like running anymore. In our sit-down, social-media–driven society, people don't do that. We drive everywhere with GPS devices built into our cars. We sit in front of a screen all day. But runners know that there is more to life than logic and technology and Twitter feeds. Just because we don't need to run doesn't mean we shouldn't. Runners instinctively know this. They understand, perhaps better than anyone, that physical effort is the path to a better, more fulfilling life.

Running is a chance to try. To make an effort. Whether it's to try to run longer, faster, easier, or smarter, there's an opportunity for every type of runner to try, from the beginner to the Olympian. If you want to become a better runner, you need to get out of your comfort zone, physically and emotionally, and make an effort that you have not made before.

There are consequences to our efforts. If we try harder, we succeed more. And success breeds motivation to try harder to succeed more. As the favorite line of many coaches and teachers goes, you get out of it what you put into it. Life is funny that way. Research has shown that individuals who learn a physical task with the belief that performance reflects inherent aptitude, as opposed to effort and practice, show little increase in self-confidence. To develop confidence, individuals must believe that their hard work and effort can lead to skill proficiency. And so my daily run becomes something of consequence. I get out of it what I put into it. And so do you.

Talented people seem to have it easier. We think they don't have to try to succeed. I have always been interested in talented people. I like hanging out with them, learning from them, being inspired by them. It seems silly on the surface. Why should I be more interested in someone just because she can run like Shalane Flanagan or he can sing like Josh Groban. After all, Shalane Flanagan can run fast because she was literally born to run fast—both of her parents were elite runners. If your parents were elite runners, you would be an elite runner, too. But there is more to it than that. Talent alone, while extremely important, isn't enough to get a runner to the Olympics or a singer to Carnegie Hall. One of the reasons I like coaching talented runners is that they are willing to do whatever it takes to achieve their goals. They don't make excuses, and they don't flake. They practice. A lot. They sacrifice. They focus on what they need to do, and they do it. They are willing to *try*.

Motivation

Scientists at Loughborough University asked 138 coaches and athletes in the United Kingdom to answer a questionnaire that measured their satisfaction with performance, instruction, and the coach-athlete relationship to find out the motivational forces on the satisfaction of coaches and athletes. One athlete from each of the coaches who participated in the study was also asked to complete the questionnaire. The scientists found that intrinsic motivation—motivation from internal factors—was positively related to all facets of coach satisfaction, while extrinsic motivation—motivation from external factors—was only related to coach satisfaction with the coach-athlete relationship. Furthermore, athletes' satisfaction with the coach-athlete relationship was associated only with the coach's intrinsic motivation. The scientists also found a significant interaction between the two types of motivation, suggesting that extrinsic motivation can potentially undermine intrinsic motivation when intrinsic motivation is low. Other research has also found that when people do not have a strong internal desire to do something, extrinsic motivation hurts the outcome. In other words, we don't run for the T-shirt or the medal or to lose the five pounds around our waistline. Not really, anyway.

For example, psychologists divided seventy-two creative writers at Brandeis University and Boston University into three groups and asked them to write poetry. After writing for a bit, the writers were given reasons to write more. The first group was given a list of extrinsic reasons for writing, such as impressing teachers, making money, and getting into graduate school, and were asked to think about their own writing with respect to these reasons. The second group was given a list of intrinsic reasons for writing, such as the enjoyment of playing with words and the satisfaction achieved from self-expression. The third group was not given any reasons for writing. The psychologists found that not only did the students who were given the extrinsic reasons write less creatively than those in the other two groups, but the quality of their work dropped significantly.

In another study, girls in the fifth and sixth grades were divided into two groups and asked to tutor younger children. One group was promised free movie tickets for teaching well, while the other group was not offered a reward. The researchers found that the tutors who were promised the reward of movie tickets were much less effective at tutoring the younger children, taking longer to communicate ideas, getting frustrated more easily, and doing a poorer job than those who were not rewarded.

Despite how shiny your marathon medal looks as it dangles from its post on your wall, the intrinsic rewards of running will always far outweigh the extrinsic ones. Sure, we all like shiny medals. But when the motivation and reason and discipline and desire to run and to be a better runner comes from inside of you, you have a much greater chance of success. When it is *you* that drives you, the process and the effort mean so much more. It becomes personal. You care about what you're doing in a way that you never do when the rewards are extrinsic. To become better runners, we must find intrinsic reasons for wanting to be better.

Inspiration

When I first started running track as a kid, my dream was to run in the Olympics. Starting out as a sprinter, I remember watching Carl Lewis on television in the 1984 Olympics in Los Angeles, repeating the four gold medals that Jesse Owens achieved at the 1936 Olympics in Berlin. I wanted to be the next Carl Lewis. He was so fast and so smooth when he ran that, after watching him, I quickly went outside my mother's house with my Puma track spikes and metal starting blocks and tried to sprint down the sidewalk from the corner of the street to the mailbox as fast as I could, my hands open and fingers outstretched, just like Carl ran.

When I started high school, I ran cross-country. Over the years, I gradually moved away from the sprints and became a distance runner, but never lost my fascination with sprinting speed and Carl Lewis. It wasn't until I watched, from a second-row, finish-line seat in Olympic Stadium, Ethiopian distance runner Haile Gebrselassie win the 10,000-meter race at the 1996 Olympics in Atlanta by outsprinting Kenya's Paul Tergat that I realized just how fast a scrawny distance runner from a third-world country could run after racing 9,900 meters. I was impressed.

Somewhere between sixth grade and reality, it occurred to me that I wasn't born with Olympic-level DNA. I wasn't able to choose parents with Olympic-caliber speed. So I never became the next Carl Lewis, nor did I ever become the next Haile Gebrselassie or any other Olympic runner, despite how many times I saw myself win an Olympic gold medal in my mind. We don't always get what we want.

Most of you, like me, will never be as fast or as powerful a runner as Carl Lewis or Haile Gebrselassie or any other elite runners. But we can be inspired by them and still derive as much pleasure and enjoyment and challenge from our running as they do from theirs, and we can still strive to be the best runners we can be.

Inspiration can come from many people, not just Olympians. It can come from a parent, a spouse, a teacher, a coach, a friend, even from yourself. It can be as ostentatious as winning a gold medal on an Olympic stage, or it can be as subtle as a tiny gesture someone makes when no one is watching. Wherever that inspiration comes from, it is ours and ours alone. Regardless of how slow or fast you are, running is the perfect outlet for that inspiration.

Thoughts

Philosopher René Descartes first wrote his famous phrase, "I think, therefore I am," in his native French: "Je pense, donc je suis," which was later published in Latin to a wider audience of scholars as "Cogito, ergo sum," because back then people actually spoke Latin. Regardless of the language, what Descartes meant, of course, is that thinking about one's existence is proof in itself that one exists to do the thinking. As Descartes himself explained, "We cannot doubt of our existence while we doubt . . ."

If I am because I think, I am surely better because I run. Runs are the best times of the day to think, to become our minds. Philosophers as far back as the ancient Greeks recognized a difference between mind and matter. Plato believed that the mind is the only true reality, the thing of greatest worth, that ideas are implanted in the mind before they are embedded in the body. Aristotle believed the two are intertwined. There can be no matter without mind, he proposed, and no mind without matter. Running blends our minds and matter, enabling us to think and become our thoughts.

When we're not running, we think about the specific things we're doing—assignments at work or school, taking our kids to soccer practice, cooking dinner. When we run, we can allow our minds to wander, letting thoughts seamlessly come and go like instruments in a symphony orchestra, dismissing those we don't need and keeping others we want to remember. I don't bring a pencil and paper with me when I run, so when I think of something I want to remember, like something I want to include in this book, I repeat the idea to myself a number of times or think of something that will make me remember it, so I can write it down once I get home. Those moments of random thoughts, some solution to a problem, or a great idea I want to write about are some of the best moments of my runs. I get excited, thinking I just found a gem.

As the Greek Stoics and Epicureans believed, we form ideas from the way we sense our experiences and learn from those sensory perceptions. Running at a pace that frees our minds, we are provided with the perfect sensory experience to think and develop ideas. Our thoughts and ideas are superbly and uniquely dependent on how we sense our movements and our perceptions of the world around us. A runner on the plains in Africa can never have the same thoughts or ideas as a runner on the city streets in America. A runner on one side of the street can never have the same thoughts or ideas as a runner on the other side of the street. The thoughts you have on your runs are *your* thoughts; no one else can ever have the same experience of thought, because our experiences and sensory perceptions are never the same. Running provides the forum for ideas to develop, manifest, and grow, offering us a unique space of intellectual freedom.

We all have an inner dialogue when we run and race. We try to convince ourselves to get out of bed to go run, that we're not as fatigued at the 21-mile mark of a marathon as we really are, that one more 800-meter rep on the track will be the difference in whether we run a PR in our next race, that if we can stay with the runner who just came up on our shoulder, we can beat him. The truth is, we can often do a lot more than we think we can. Running is one of the best ways to prove it to ourselves and anyone else who may be watching. Many times I have coached a runner to do one more rep at the end of her interval workout when she thought she was done. Running is so objective, so precise, so finite in its measurement. Can I pick up the pace right now? Can I pass that runner before the finish line? Can I run one more rep and run it faster than the last one? The answer is either yes or no. We can see the result of our thoughts and our internal dialogue. We can see the result of our actions. And we must live with the result.

When I run fast, my thoughts and the way I think change from when I run slowly—I become more focused on my body, on the effort I'm putting forth, and what it feels like. Some runners are natural associative thinkers—they focus on the action of running and the discomfort of all-out effort. Other runners are natural dissociative thinkers—they focus on something else to get their mind off the action of running and the discomfort of the effort. I've always been an associative thinker. During a hard tempo run, interval workout, or race, I turn inward. My attention goes to the effort itself. I think about what my body is doing—the rhythm of my breathing, the cadence of my legs, my arm swing. I think about trying to pop off the ground with each step like the Kenyans, whose feet pop off the ground as if they were landing on hot coals.

Research has shown that I'm not alone in this relationship between effort and thoughts. A study from Northumbria University in the United Kingdom examined the effect of low- and high-intensity running on runners' thoughts—what the scientists called the "inner dialogue"—and its relationship to the runners' rating of perceived exertion (RPE). When running at a low intensity (50 percent of peak running speed) and RPE, runners' thoughts were dissociative—they thought about things other than the running that they were doing. When running at a high intensity (70 percent of peak running speed) and RPE, runners' thoughts were associative—they thought about what their bodies were doing and the effort of their run. The scientists concluded that an athlete's "internal dialogue" is intensity-dependent, and may relate to the more urgent need to self-monitor physical changes and sensations when running at a high intensity.

It's a weird way to think, to focus on the discomfort itself. I don't know why I think this way. I don't try to; it just happens. Given humans' proclivity toward self-preservation, one would think that the natural tendency would be to focus on something other than the discomfort. I know so many runners who are dissociative thinkers who run with music to get their minds off the effort of their runs.

Discomfort

I used to coach a recent college graduate who commented on the fact that many of the best college distance-running teams in the US are based in cold climates. He believed this was more than coincidence, because he thought that running in cold, icy, snowy weather makes runners tougher. Anyone can run when the weather is nice, after all. But it takes a warrior to brave the elements and run outside in cold climates. I'm not sure if I agree that running in the cold makes you a better runner, but it certainly demands something of you that more temperate climates don't. Successful runners have a certain toughness about them, a willingness to be uncomfortable, to train despite less-than-ideal climatic conditions. While that toughness, like certain physiological traits, is largely genetic, you can acquire toughness through training, as you become more capable of tolerating high degrees of physical discomfort. While running easy every day is easy, don't shy away from difficult workouts, even in the rain or the cold, as they will help you develop the toughness you need to become a better runner and handle life's difficulties.

At a recent track meet, I was talking to a fellow runner in his fifties before the start of our race. He told me, "After all these years, I still get nervous before every race." I smiled and responded, "That's because you know it's going to be uncomfortable." To which he responded, "That's a big part of it."

Runners do something very unique—we seek out discomfort. Yet we get nervous and anxious about it. Every interval workout and every race is physically and even emotionally uncomfortable. After you get past a certain point, whether with your total running experience or your specific workout on Tuesday, that's all there really is. Runners deal in discomfort. It's our currency. The million-dollar question is why do we do this? Why do we put ourselves in a position in which we're going to be physically uncomfortable, especially when we know the anxiousness and nervousness and physical symptoms it causes? Most people go through every day of their lives never experiencing what that feels like.

The answer, at least for me, is quite long and difficult for non-runners to understand. Sometimes, it is even difficult for me to understand. I am reminded of what Friedrich Nietzsche said: "He who has a *why* to live for can bear with almost any *how*." The self-exploration, the complete and utter freedom of all-out physical effort is my *why*. It makes me feel alive. The anxiousness that preempts the discomfort keeps me on that razor's edge—just enough to make me aware of my thoughts and feelings, to know that I am human, yet not so much that it incapacitates my ability to perform.

We learn about ourselves when we're uncomfortable. One of the things I learned very early in my running life is that running forces you to learn about yourself in ways that you just can't get in the rest of your life. During those moments in every race, in every interval workout, when it's physically uncomfortable, we are presented with a question: Do we back off from the discomfort of the pace to make it hurt less, or do we meet that discomfort with all of the courage we have and push through it to achieve the result we want to achieve and learn about ourselves in a very unique and extraordinary way? We are asked in no uncertain terms, "What are you going to do right now?" Few other times in our lives are we asked such a decisive question at such a decisive moment. It's very revealing. Sometimes, we find out things about ourselves we can be immensely proud of. We are proud of ourselves for dealing with the discomfort in a positive way, to rise above something uncomfortable to find something extraordinary. Other times, we find out things about ourselves that are less desirable, things we would rather not admit, things we don't really want to know. It is in those revealing moments that we learn about how we handle difficult situations. For better and for worse, we get to know who we are. If we fail or disappoint ourselves, we can make a pact with ourselves to handle those situations better next time. When I'm in the middle of a workout, I often think about how I'm going to feel after it's over, that sense of calm and pride that washes over me in the moments afterward, when I get to bask in the glow of what I have just completed, when I can take a look back at the track as I leave the stadium and say, "I defeated *you* today." But that is not enough. I must *earn* the calm and the pride. As it is written in the book of Romans (5:3–5): ". . . we rejoice in our sufferings, knowing that suffering produces endurance, and endurance produces character, and character produces hope . . ."

Running gives us the opportunity to seek out discomfort so that we may learn to deal with it, rise above it, and become hopeful about our future. And that's very much like life. Just like in running, there are moments in life that are difficult and test our resolve. When we are faced with problems, when we are faced with an enormous amount of stress, do we back off and hide under the bedsheets, or do we meet that problem or that challenge head on?

The trick to running, if there is a trick, is to become comfortable with being uncomfortable. How do you do that? By subjecting your body to the training. By running more miles, by running more miles faster, by pushing yourself just a little harder in the last two miles of your long run, by trying just a little harder on the next-to-last rep of the interval workout, rather than waiting for the last rep. Runners accept that the race will hurt and look at it as a challenge to become the courageous people they want to be. Be courageous with your running. The encounter with discomfort is purifying. It allows us to test the strength of our will by providing an obstacle, and we learn to what extent we are in control of ourselves.

Belief

I don't always love everything about running. Some workouts are downright difficult, and I'd prefer not to do them. Long tempo runs and long interval workouts, like 800-meter to mile reps, have always been difficult for me. But I do those workouts, because I believe they will make me a better runner. I feel a sense of pride when I get the workout out of me and onto the track or the road. I go from potential energy (I think I can do this) to kinetic energy (I'm doing it). At the end of the workout, at the end of the day, that's what this running process is all about—becoming a better runner and a better you, and not being afraid of or timid about doing something that's difficult. We can gain strength from running. Physical strength. Emotional strength. Mindful strength. Spiritual strength. But we have to believe it's possible.

I often tell myself, as I suspect many runners do, that the discomfort of doing a hard interval workout or tempo run, or of running ten miles in the heat, will be worth it when it's time to go to the starting line ready to race. I've run in both very hot and very cold weather many times in my life and have done innumerable hard workouts, and I ask myself, "Why am I doing this? Why run under the hot sun? Why put myself through such discomfort all the time?" But of course I already know the answer before I ask myself the question: Because it will be worth it. Runners run the miles in the heat and the intervals on the track, because we believe it will be worth it. We tell ourselves, "By doing this workout, it will help me when I go to the starting line."

But it may not. There are no guarantees, after all. Despite the miles in the heat or the rain or the snow, despite the hard workouts, despite all of the discomfort that goes into the training, we may still not get the result we are chasing. That's life. I've never been as fast as I've wanted to be, nor have most runners I know. But in those moments of discomfort, we believe it's worth it. We hold on to the belief, because that's all we really have. We don't know what will happen tomorrow. But we have to believe that anything is possible.

The great British runner Herb Elliot once said after winning the Olympic gold medal and breaking the world 1,500-meter record, "To run a world record, you must have the absolute arrogance to think you can run a mile faster that anyone who ever lived, and then you have to have the absolute humility to actually do it." While few of us are in a position to set a world record, we all have to maintain that balance of both arrogance and humility. When you are trying to accomplish something that you have never been able to do before, whether it is running a marathon, owning a business, or writing a book, you have to believe that you are better than the self you are now. That's a step above confidence. If you want to do something that means competing against others, like getting your dream job or winning an award, you have to believe that you are better than everyone else who has applied for the job or the award. And then you have to balance that arrogance with the humility it takes to do the work worthy of it.

Competition

On a downhill portion about nine miles into a recent 12-mile run by myself, a runner with gray facial scruff and a ponytail—who looked liked he had been around the block more than a few times in his life—came up on my shoulder and passed me from behind. At first, I just let him pass since I was just running easy that day. Then something happened inside me, and I changed my mind. I picked up the pace and decided to follow him down the hill. About a couple hundred meters after we had reached the bottom of the hill and were running on the flat, I passed him. At first, it felt good, I admit, to use him on the downhill and then go past him, but almost immediately, I decided to wave at him to come up to me, so we could run together. At first, he declined.

"You're running too fast," he said between audible breaths.

"Come on, we'll help each other out." I said.

He obliged.

For the next mile or so, we ran side-by-side, cruising along the wood-chipped trail at a much faster pace than what I had been running just a minute earlier. And it felt good. I noticed he had an accent. I asked him where he was from. "Ireland," he replied. Funny, I thought, it being the day before St. Patrick's Day. Perhaps this was a sign? I started talking to him.

"What's your name?" I asked.

"Raymond."

"Nice to meet you, Raymond. I'm Jason."

"Nice to meet you, Jason."

We kept talking for most of the mile we ran together. He told me he runs five miles each day on this wood-chipped trail, after being a smoker for thirty years. "I do this for my health," he said.

I turned a corner to run a few more miles on my own down another road as we finished Raymond's five-mile path. I said goodbye to my new Irish friend with the scruffy face and ponytail, and I thought how great it felt to pick up the pace and cruise on the trail with someone who could push me, and how we helped each other run faster than we could or would have run on our own.

It's hard to find a runner who isn't competitive, if only with him or herself. Every runner—from the 2:04 marathoner to the 5:04 marathoner, and the 4-minute miler to the 8-minute miler—wants to get faster. And it feels good to beat someone else. But it also feels good to cooperate. And that's just the point. When we help others, we make ourselves feel good. We help ourselves. Darwin was right after all. Human behaviors are not purely altruistic. They are inherently selfish, because natural selection favors selfish behavior to increase our reproductive success. We don't truly help others to help *them*. We help them to help *ourselves*.

Regardless of the motivating factor behind my reason for waving to Raymond to pick up the pace and run with me, we both benefitted from it. Maybe I did it for me, or maybe I did it for him. Or maybe I did it for some reason that had nothing to do with either of us. I don't really know. All I know is that it felt like the right thing to do at that moment. It was, in a word, fun. Next time a runner comes up on your shoulder during a run, pick up the pace and run together. Help each other achieve something that you both wouldn't or couldn't achieve on your own.

Wherever you are, Raymond from Ireland, thank you. You made my day.

In March of 2011, I was in Napa Valley, California, for a book signing and to speak at the Napa Valley Marathon race expo. Two of the other guest speakers were four-time New York City Marathon and four-time Boston Marathon winner Bill Rodgers and Olympic Marathon gold medalist Joan Benoit Samuelson. I had met Bill before, but this was my first time meeting Joan.

We were all staying at a quaint inn among the vineyards of the valley. After the event was over, I did what any runner would do—I asked them to go for a run the next morning before we headed to the airport to catch our flights home. Bill said, "Sure." Joan wasn't so sure, but said she might join us. When I got up at 6:00 a.m., Bill was waiting for me in the inn's lobby. But no sign of Joan. I wasn't about to knock on the door of an Olympic gold medalist to urge her to run with us, and I wasn't going to ask Bill to do it, so Bill and I left and started our run. We hadn't run five minutes when we heard someone approaching us from behind. We stopped to wait for her.

"Why did you stop?" Joan asked, as she continued running right past us to take the lead.

We continued to run together, past vineyards that lined both sides of the country road, with Joan always a step in front. After four and a half miles, we decided it was time to turn around and head back to the inn.

As we approached the street sign that we designated as our turnaround point, I sensed that Joan was going to pick up the pace. She had just run twenty miles of the marathon the day before as a training run, but I could just feel that she was about to do something. Sure enough, as soon as we turned around, she picked up the pace and held it for the remaining four and a half miles back to the inn, with Bill and I left to decide what we were going to do. So we picked up the pace, too, of course. We spent the next four and a half miles cruising down the solitary road through the beautiful Napa Valley countryside, the faint smell of wine mixing with that of the pine trees. Given all of the places she's run in the world, I asked Joan where her favorite place to run has been. "Right here, right now," she said.

Later that morning, after we had showered and eaten breakfast, Bill and I left for the airport. Joan stayed at the inn, because her flight was later in the day. As Bill and I were talking in the car, he asked, "Did you notice that Joan picked up the pace?"

"Not only did I notice, I anticipated it," I responded. I was pretty proud of myself.

I knew of Joan's competitive reputation. And of course Bill knew it, too. He's pretty competitive himself, even in his sixties.

One has to be fiercely competitive to win the New York City Marathon and Boston Marathon four times each. And one has to be fiercely competitive to win the Olympic Marathon, especially when it's the first Olympic Marathon that women had ever run. Whomever won that race was going to be the trailblazer.

No matter what level of runner you are, you need competition from others. I became a better runner that day on that quiet country road in Napa Valley because of Bill Rodgers and Joan Benoit Samuelson. But also because something instinctual made me want to compete. Our truest competitor lies deep within us.

Destiny

I have a friend who thinks I, like other hardcore runners, am self-absorbed and elitist, that I am all about running all the time, that nothing else matters, and that if you don't run yourself, you are judged as less than someone who does. She is not alone in her opinion. What bothers many people about runners is our almost arrogant attitude that we are somehow better than everyone else because we run and that by running we are somehow fulfilling some grand destiny. We look at people who don't run as somehow inferior because their resting heart rate is not below fifty, and as somehow complacent because they're not willing to push themselves physically for the pursuit of a faster time on a stopwatch. We wonder when they are going to have a heart attack.

It doesn't take long for non-runners to figure out that runners are indeed a different breed. We spend a lot of time reflecting on our runs and races. We talk about PRs and whether a run felt good or bad. We lay out our clothes on the floor the night before a race like a five-year-old preparing for school tomorrow. We spread a substance called Body Glide on our groin and nipples to prevent chafing during long runs. Most runners are a bit crazy.

Runners have an obsession with running that rivals most other obsessions, perhaps because runners truly believe that they are running toward who they want to be, toward some panacea. For me, and I suspect for many other runners, running narrows the gap between who I am and who I can be, between my reality and my aspirations. If Body Glide helps me to become the person I aspire to be, so be it.

People should do whatever exercise they want to do, as long as they do something. People don't *have* to run. I guess I'm guilty of believing that if people ran, their lives—and the world—would be much better. I really do believe that. There is something about runners' approach to running and life—and their search for meaning in their running and life— that distinguishes them from all other people who exercise. Problems are solved on runs. Running gives us the promise of hope for a better future. If the world's political leaders ran together for their meetings, and the rest of the public followed their lead, the world would indeed be a better place.

With all of the running I've done over the years, I've been asked many times what I'm running away from. People, especially non-runners, seem to think that because I run a lot, I must be running away from something. Why else would I run so much? Their question always startles me, because I've always seen myself as running *toward* something. What it is that I'm running toward I'm not always sure. However, it's usually toward getting faster. This was certainly the case when I was younger and my fastest races were still in my future. I always wanted to be faster. The challenge of getting faster was thrilling. Over the years and through different phases of my life, what I'm running toward has changed.

Lately, I've been running back toward my youth, chasing the times of my younger running self. But, being in my early forties, I reluctantly realize that my fastest races are behind me, and I have to find new meaning for my running. I'm still trying to get faster, to get at least within arm's reach of the times of my youth, but now my running is about getting faster relative to my age and how fast I am today, rather than to my personal records I ran in my twenties. It's humbling to say the least. When I race now, I can't help but compare my times to what I used to run. It bothers me that I am running slower than I used to. When I run a bad race, and I don't feel sharp, it negatively affects me. I don't feel good about myself. "Why do I feel this way?" I ask myself. "It's just running." Ultimately, in life's bigger picture, running is just an activity I choose to do. It shouldn't define my self worth. Yet it does, and I am perplexed as to *why*. I suspect that other runners feel the same way. Are runners so self-absorbed—am *I* so self-absorbed—that I cannot feel good about myself if my running is not going well? Has this been my destiny all along? Running gives a lot of people confidence. It's why I included it as a chapter in this book. For me, however, that confidence is too often tied to how fast I run and now, in my forties, tied to a comparison of how fast my races used to be and how fast I used to feel. When I run fast, when I *feel* fast, it creates a powerful confidence that penetrates everything else I do. I feel on top of the world. I post pictures on Facebook and Instagram of me racing and include clever and inspirational captions for my followers. Somehow, being physically fit and fast influences the way I feel about myself and my outlook on the world. It gives me a sense of achievement. For most of us, our confidence is intimately connected to our physical being, because we live through our bodies. So when I run slower than I want or than I used to, when I don't *feel* fast, my confidence wavers. I don't post any pictures on social media and don't even tell anyone I ran a race. I don't feel like I have achieved. I drive home by myself and overanalyze what just happened. I want to be left alone.

Of course, I can choose to be confident or not. A person's confidence shouldn't be tied to how fast a race is run. We are not destined to let trivial things define who we are. That we often do may reveal a flaw in our design. Or it may reveal one of the cleverest characteristics that distinguish humans from all other animals—the urge to be *better*. No matter how fast or slow we are today, we all have the ability to decide we will try harder, to be better tomorrow, to affect our destiny. That's why runners are so special—because we have an acutely measurable way to know where we are now, and we make the decision to try to be better tomorrow. Every runner, whether a twenty-five-year-old world-record holder or an eighty-five-year-old who finishes last in the race—wants to be faster, wants to strive for some better version of himself or herself. *That* is our destiny.

But it's not that simple. I can't say that I'm running solely because I want to get faster. I do, but that's not the entire reason. That's not what gets me out the door every day to run. I suppose, when I think hard enough about it, I *am* running away from something. I'm running away from becoming the person I *don't* want to be. I don't want to be that overweight, slow, out-of-shape, lazy guy who sits in his La-Z-Boy chair or on a sports-bar stool and watches football all day Sunday in his undershirt. I don't want to be the middle-aged man who looks himself in the mirror and wonders where the good-looking high-school athlete went, deciding to run a marathon to cure his midlife crisis. I don't want to be the person who takes the easy way out and never challenges himself. I don't want to be the person who lives an ordinary life. So I run away from it. All of it. I run away from becoming lazy. I run away from the guilt of not running. I run away from a bad race I had last weekend. I run away from becoming normal and ordinary. I run away from all of the things I don't like about myself. I run away from complacency.

We all have things we run toward or away from. I've met runners who run toward life, toward freedom, health, and friendships, toward love, toward happiness. And I've met runners who run away from obesity, from family, relationships, and divorce, from drugs, from depression, from heart disease and cancer. When we run, we are free of those things. We are free from what binds us, from what keeps us down, from what holds us back. Running helps us cope—with tragedy, with disappointment, with frustration, with sadness, with all of the negative feelings that hold us back from living a happy, fulfilling life. Whether it's thousands of people running 26.2 miles through the streets of Boston for a common goal, or just you running three miles alone around your block before work, running, on both a large, public scale and a small, personal scale, gives us hope for our future. What are *you* running away from? What are *you* running toward?

Potential

A few years ago, I was having a conversation with a runner after she had just run a half-marathon. She said she was disappointed with her time. Not far from us stood the runner who won the race, her long, sculpted legs glowing in the sun as she ate her post-race banana. The runner I was talking to gestured to the winner and commented in exasperation, "Why can't I run as fast as her?" It's a question many runners ponder. Including me.

"Because you don't have her parents," I responded. Perhaps it wasn't the best thing for a coach to say at that moment, however true it may be.

One of the most difficult lessons I have learned about running is that we should not compare ourselves to how fast other runners are. Runners do this all the time. It's too easy to do so. I've done it my whole life. Every time you run a race, there will be other runners who beat you. Only one person wins. It doesn't even have to be the winner of the race that we compare ourselves to. It could be the guy in your local running group or your girlfriend who travels with you to every race. When you run with other people, it doesn't take long to notice that some runners are clearly faster than others. We're not all created equal. So it's very easy to say, "I wish I was as fast as he/she is." But unless you have the same parents, and therefore the same DNA, as that other runner, it is only self-defeating to compare yourself to him or her. This comparison problem is unique to humans. Only humans compare themselves to other members of their species. Cheetahs don't say to themselves, "I wish I was as fast as that spotted cheetah in my running group." Cheetahs don't know how to compare. They just run.

People ask me why I love to coach. The superficial, yet also true, answer is that I love applying the science in such a way that it helps runners get faster and achieve their goals. The deeper, yet more difficult to articulate, answer is that it fills me up inside to help a runner create a performance that he or she previously couldn't have created or didn't think was possible. Whether I'm coaching a beginner to learn how to run, a runner to PR at her next marathon, a high-school miler to break five minutes, or an elite runner to qualify for the Olympic Trials, I feel a deep satisfaction in the coaching process. When I stand near the start line of my runners' races, I feel the same nervous excitement as when I'm about to run the race myself. There have been many times I have become overwhelmed with emotion when watching my athletes run and seeing them achieve their potential.

Being a better runner isn't just about running faster. After all, we all have limits to how good of a runner we can be. Those limits are set by our DNA, and there's little we can do about that. What is important is not how fast we become, but how close to our own potential we can get. For it is in that relentless pursuit of our own individual greatness where the true value lies. The lessons you learn about yourself, the ability to stand up to your fears and your hopes, and the act of *trying* to become better, that is what running is all about. It is what gets you out the door at 6:00 a.m. before heading to the office. It's what makes you go to bed early on a Saturday night so you can be ready to do a long run on Sunday morning. It's what makes you search out for the best Italian restaurants when you travel so you can refuel for your runs. It's what makes you laugh at the word *fartlek*.

Runners are always in process. We are always preparing for a race, always training for something bigger than ourselves, involved in the means not simply to make them meet at the ends, but for the value in the means themselves.

So just run. Use faster runners as inspiration, to prompt you to work harder and be better. But don't compare yourself to them. Compare yourself to *you*, and try to be better tomorrow and next week and next month and next year than you are today. Meet your potential. If you look yourself in the mirror and you can say you are doing everything possible to be better, then you have succeeded. We can be only as fast as our DNA allows. What you can be proud of is doing everything possible to meet the potential of your DNA.

Risk

I've been talking to a talented runner where I live in San Diego for a couple of years about working with me as her coach. She waffles back and forth about going through with it. Part of all her waffling, she says, is financial—she can't afford to hire a coach. But even when I have offered to coach her pro bono, because she's got so much potential, she still waffles. She told me that she's afraid of failure.

Humans have a bad habit. We get in our own way. We perceive that external obstacles prevent us from accomplishing our dreams. We let our fears, our lack of faith, our thoughts, and our emotions control our actions. But it's often the obstacles that lie within us that prevent us from meeting our potential. Many of us stop short of pursuing our dreams or following through with something because we're afraid of failing. With greater success comes greater expectations, and then what if we're not good enough to meet those expectations? It's become too easy in our society to be complacent and maintain the status quo. And why not be complacent? When everyone receives a medal at the end of a race, regardless of place or time, it seems that everyone is a winner these days. We reward mediocrity instead of challenging and inspiring people to be better.

As an entrepreneur, I spend a lot of time thinking about the process of accomplishment. I've always been drawn to people with talent, but even more so to people who are willing to completely commit to doing whatever it takes to accomplish what they want to accomplish, however real the risk of failure may be.

Running inherently has risk. It's too objective not to. You either finish the marathon or you don't. You either get faster or you don't. Stopwatches don't lie. We can't go through life crying over spilled almond milk, wishing that we were something that we're not. It's easy to say, "If only I could do this," or "If only I were able to do that." Some of us are faster runners than others. Some of us are smarter than others. Some of us are better looking than others. Deal with it. We are who we are, and we must accept that and try to be better tomorrow. That's all we can ask of ourselves.

While there may be a chance of failing, people take risks because the chance of failing makes success taste even sweeter. On runs, we are reminded of what poet T.S. Eliot said: "Only those who will risk going too far can possibly find out how far one can go." So take a few risks. Gain strength and momentum from your runs to help see those risks through. When you walk out your door each day to run, remind yourself who you want to be and what you want to accomplish. Use each run and each workout to help you be that person and accomplish those things. Commit to running and commit to becoming a better person. If you want something you've never had, you must do something you've never done.

The commitment to become a better runner is no less than a lesson in success—not just at running, but at *anything*. Every run presents a different experience, a different challenge, a different chance to accomplish something that day. Running asks something of you that you are very rarely asked. And if you meet that challenge head on, you'll be amazed at what you can learn about yourself and what it takes to look inward and become who you want to be. Running has the power, if you let it, to make you a better person. Running gives you a chance to discover and challenge yourself and, in so doing, become someone better than you currently are.

Challenge

With all of the technology and amenities and surplus we have in our Western culture, we can go through most of our lives and never find out how far we can be pushed, how much we can endure, how much we can handle. Our lives are pretty easy, and they are getting easier with every generation. The comforts of life are becoming more comfortable. Soon, we'll have robots to do everything for us. We'll never have to lift a finger, much less our legs.

On what may initially seem like a small scale because of its simple nature, running can teach us how much we can push ourselves and how much we can handle. But when we look deeper, we realize that it is not on such a small scale after all that we learn this from running. It is rather on a large scale, in part because the lessons are so blatant and so accessible—we have the opportunity to learn these things about ourselves on any weekend that we sign up for a race. In a very deliberate way, we can find out how much we can handle simply by lacing our shoes and running out the door. We don't have to wait for our resolve to be tested by tragedy, for some illness or accident to happen to us or our loved ones. All we have to do is run. We seek it out rather than have it inflicted on us. We own it. We take responsibility for it. And therein lies the key difference. Running can test and reveal our resolve, our courage, our endurance. And we have the choice to learn just how far we can be pushed, how much we can endure, how much we can handle. We can conquer the cowardice in ourselves.

If you hung out near the Peddie School pool in 1989–1990, you would have thought you were at the practice session of the U.S. Olympic Team. The intensity and focus were palpable. And you might have overheard Chris Martin, the coach of the

Peddie swim team, say to B.J. (Bedford) Miller and the rest of his swimmers, "If it doesn't hurt, you're not doing it right." Good coaches often know just what to say.

Interval workouts and racing, if you do them correctly, inherently include discomfort. What makes the swimmers at the Peddie School in the small town of Hightstown different is not simply the chlorine smell of their hair and immense talent, but that they seek out discomfort every day in the pool, because they want to be the best swimmers in the world.

"Coach Martin brought out the best in us by pushing us beyond where we believed we could go," B.J. nostalgically says now, twenty-five years later. "He had high expectations, and none of us wanted to let him down. He figured out how to motivate each of us, either by yelling or by persuading, or whatever it was going to take."

"The training was hard. Some of the hardest training I've ever done. Arguably the hardest, although the training I did later was different. There was more honing later, but what Coach Martin provided was the platform to be great. I always say Peddie was a great place to be from. While there, I suffered through a lot of it, but having it as where I came from changed my life. And at the end of the season, I could stand on the starting blocks and know there wasn't a soul out there who had worked harder than me. There's a lot to that. Ultimately, Coach Martin gave me the shoulders to stand on to achieve my dreams—and the shoulders turned out to be my own."

Most of us cannot be the best in the world at something. Few people win Olympic gold medals like my talented, chlorine-smelling, high-school classmates. But we can all strive to be better than we were yesterday. And we can all put our hearts into something to see what we can become, despite the fear of failure. We all have shoulders that are stronger than we may think. Running gives us the chance to stand on them. Running teaches us that we are better than we think we are and capable of going further than we thought we could . . . in running *and* in life. That alone is worth the price of enough pairs of running shoes to last a lifetime of running.

So run. Run often. Run slowly or run fast. Run one mile or run 26.2 miles. Run at 14-minute mile pace or run at 4-minute mile pace. Run continuously for thirty minutes or alternate running for five minutes and walking for five minutes. Run to be creative. Run to be imaginative. Run to be productive. Run to be confident. Run to build friendships. Run to be healthful. Just run. And during those slow runs and fast runs and short runs and long runs, you'll find your inner runner, and in so doing, you'll discover who you are and who you can become. You'll create a world of magic inside of you. And when that happens, the world—and you—is full of possibilities.

ABOUT THE AUTHOR

Arunner since age eleven and a philosopher since age twelve, Dr. Jason Karp is one of America's foremost running experts, an entrepreneur, and the creator of the Revo₂lution Running™ certification. He owns Run-Fit, the premier provider of innovative running and fitness services. He has been profiled in a number of publications and is the 2011 IDEA Personal Trainer of the Year (the fitness industry's highest award) and 2014 recipient of the President's Council on Fitness, Sports, & Nutrition Community Leadership Award.

Dr. Karp has given dozens of international lectures and has been a featured speaker at most of the world's top fitness conferences and coaching clinics, including Asia Fitness Convention, Indonesia Fitness &

Jody Lynn Photography

Health Expo, FILEX Fitness Convention, U.S. Track & Field and Cross Country Coaches Association Convention, American College of Sports Medicine Conference, IDEA World Fitness Convention, National Strength and Conditioning Association Conference, and CanFitPro, among others. He has taught USA Track & Field's highest-level coaching certification and has led coaching camps at the U.S. Olympic Training Center.

A prolific writer, Jason has more than 200 articles published in numerous international coaching, running, and fitness magazines, including *Track Coach*, *Techniques for Track & Field and Cross Country*, *New Studies in Athletics*, *Runner's World*, *Running Times*, *Women's Running*, *Marathon & Beyond*, *IDEA Fitness Journal*, *Oxygen*, *SELF*, *Shape*, and *Active.com*, among others. He is also the author of five other books: *Running a Marathon For Dummies*, *Running for Women*, *101 Winning Racing Strategies for Runners*, *101 Developmental Concepts & Workouts for Cross Country Runners*, and *How to Survive Your PhD*, and is the editor of the sixth edition of *Track & Field Omnibook*.

At age twenty-four, Dr. Karp became one of the youngest college head coaches in the country, leading the Georgian Court University women's cross-country team to the regional championship and winning honors as NAIA Northeast Region Coach of the Year. He has also coached high-school track and field and cross-country. As a personal trainer, he has worked with clients ranging from elite athletes to cardiac-rehab patients. As a private coach, he has helped many runners meet their potential, ranging from a first-time race participant to an Olympic Trials qualifier. A competitive runner since sixth grade, Dr. Karp is a nationally certified running coach through USA Track & Field, has been sponsored by PowerBar and Brooks, and was a member of the silver-medal–winning United States masters half-marathon team at the 2013 World Maccabiah Games in Israel.

Dr. Karp received his PhD in exercise physiology with a physiology minor from Indiana University in 2007, his master's degree in kinesiology from the University of Calgary in 1997, and his bachelor's degree in exercise and sport science with an English minor from Penn State University in 1995. His research has been published in the scientific journals *Medicine & Science in Sports & Exercise, International Journal of Sport Nutrition and Exercise Metabolism,* and *International Journal of Sports Physiology and Performance.*